VICTORIOUS FAITH

In a Broken World

Arlin Sanford

ISBN 978-1-960903-37-2 (Ebook)

ISBN 978-1-960903-38-9 (Paperback)

ISBN 978-1-960903-39-6 (Hardcover)

Publify Publishing

1412 W. Ave B

Lampasas, TX 76550

publifypublishing@gmail.com

Acknowledgements

The Lord God Almighty

Inspiration and direction to the "*author and perfecter of faith*" (Heb.12:2)

Wife, Lana Sanford

Illustrating the cover for this publication Patience during the time of the writing of this book.

Brother Douglas Sanford

Putting together the Bible study questions for the readers to journal their life of faith.

Introduction

Our attention is captured by the writer of Hebrews (Heb.11:6) in penning:

"*Without faith it is impossible to please* Him (God)"; all must evaluate their own 'faith walk' before the Lord. We, as believers in our world, should be sincere about "pleasing" God – it is to be a priority. Any who are diligently "*seeking first the Kingdom of God and His righteousness*" (Mt.6:33) will be compelled to recognize the priority that 'faith' is placed in the Scriptures. Our salvation is founded upon the fact it's by God's "*grace we have been saved though* (our) *faith.* (Eph.2:8,9)"

The Scribe of Hebrews presents us with many testimonies from "*men of old*" who were faced with dilemmas requiring decisions on their part that allowed them to be partakers of unexpected happenings never before witnessed. Trusting in the unseen, while not being sure of the outcome – other than with absolute assurance that whatever God divulged - could be responded to as truth.

We are living in a time, in a broken world, where many questions are asked as to where our culture is going. What's around the corner? Can things get worse? Are we in danger?

In these uncertain days it would be prudent to emulate three servants of the Lord who found themselves in a hot spot.

Shadrach, Meshach, and Aben-nego (Dan.3:13-18) had made a commitment before the Lord to remain obedient under any circumstance. It brought them to a place where a decision must be made - Bow or Suffer!

Their 'faith' shouted out; "We are willing to suffer!" They stated, "*our God whom we serve is able to deliver* us from *the blazing fire…but even if He does not….we are not going* to serve or *worship the golden image.*" Of course, God did deliver them from the fire; there wasn't even a trace of smoke.

This is an example of the type of faith needed for today, and the type of faith we will be exhibiting in this book. I encourage you to read carefully each text and meditate on the discourse. Then, carefully chronicle your own thoughts as to where you see your "Faith Walk" going. I'm praying for you as you grow in faith and in the Lord.

Questions or comments: kingdomliving17@yahoo.com

Pastor Arlin Sanford

For we students of the Bible 'faith' is a subject that thoroughly captivates our attention. Why wouldn't it? Verses like: "*The righteous (Just) man shall live by faith*" (*Gal.* 3:11), *and* "*without faith it is impossible to please* (God)" (*Heb*..11:6), becomes a driving force to "*hear...the word of Christ*" (*Rom*.10:17) and grow in faith.

As one grows in faith, accounts of their steadfast character will become those that testify of their diligence in magnifying reliance upon the Lord instead of oneself. This publication will deal with the stories of "Faith' found in Hebrews 11 = the faith chapter. The writer of these Scriptures gives us some incredible illustrations of God's servants. Contained within the narrative lessons are taught and biblical principles are spotlighting godly direction for the studier.

Accompanying the biblical references, we will sprinkle the dialogue with stories of faith taken from family situations. Our Lord has been so faithful over the years "*causing all things to work together for good*" (Rom.8:28). Perhaps you will be encouraged as the Word and these words bless your soul.

Also, you will find questions at the end of each chapter you can muse over and respond to the situations presented. They will help you to evaluate your level of 'faith'; then allow you to look back at your answers a year or two later and see how you've grown in your 'faith' walk.

CONTENTS

CHAPTER ONE – "Faith is Characterized " Heb. 11: 1-3 1

CHAPTER TWO - "Faith Humbles Itself Under God's Authority" Heb. 11: 4 14

CHAPTER THREE – "Ultimate Faith Prompts God to Expand the Ordinary " Heb. 11: 5, 6...27

CHAPTER FOUR - Faith That Willingly Stands Alone " Heb. 11: 7..39

CHAPTER FIVE – " Abraham's Life Reveals How One Grows in Faith " Heb. 11: 8-10...51

CHAPTER SIX – "Parents Bolster Faith in Children " Heb. 11: 17-19 62

CHAPTER SEVEN – " Faith Discerns God's Activity " Heb. 11: 21,22 73

CHAPTER EIGHT – " Faith Makes the Difficult Choices Seem Easy " Heb. 11:23-29 87

CHAPTER NINE – " Faith Fosters Unlimited Possibilities " Heb. 11: 30 104

CHAPTER TEN – " Faith Flows from The Least Expected " Heb. 11: 32-34 115

CHAPTER ELEVEN – " Ultimate Living for People of Faith " Heb. 11:35-40 135

About the Author..147

CHAPTER ONE

Heb. 11: 1 - 3

" Faith is Characterized "

You are probably familiar with, and been blessed by, the poem written by Margaret Fishback Powers called "Footprints in the Sand." If so, you'll recall the theme being that there were two sets of 'footprints' while walking beside the Lord in fellowship with Him. But when life's challenges pressed down upon her, she noticed only one 'set of footprints.' Inquiring of the Lord, "Where were You in my 'troublesome' situations?" She was told by the Lord, "that was when I was carrying you."

This, obviously, is a wonderful and inspiring written picture of the love and grace and mercy of our Lord; and has ministered to many over the years. Plus, it is so true that God has said "*I will never desert you, nor will I ever forsake you.*" (Heb.13:5) Now, while I agree with and understand the principle; I submit that, at times, God will allow us to continue walking, so that in a deeper way, and perhaps a more memorial way, walking by faith and not by sight is required.

We have an example in Matthew 14: 22-33. The sea was" *battered by the waves*" (vs.24); it was early in the morning and still dark. The disciples saw Jesus "*walking on the water, and they were frightened.*" (vs.26) Peter, asserting himself to verify it was indeed the Lord, "*got out of the boat, and walked on the water and came toward Jesus.*" (vs.27-29) Peter, much like us at times, took his eyes off the Savior, and was overtaken by the "wind.... *Became afraid, and began to sink... and cried out, 'Lord, save me!'*" (vs.30) Jesus, rich in mercy, "*stretched out his hand and took hold of him, and said, 'O you of little faith, why did you doubt?'*" (vs.31) We are told then "*they got into the boat*". Every indication we have is that Peter, was not carried, but encouraged to 'walk on the water' beside Jesus to the boat. Of course, Jesus "never left him, He didn't forsake him" but Peter needed to grasp the fullness of the lesson that would minister to him throughout his life of ministry to the masses.

Instead of giving us a 'definition' of faith, the writer of Hebrews (whose identity is subject to opinion, and not necessary to debate here) embraces the 'character' of faith for our contemplation. Describing the nuances emphasizing the level of one's trust. The depth, the steadfastness, and capacity to endure through life's entanglements without 'doubting.' He pens, "*Now faith is the assurance of things hoped for, the conviction (evidence) of things not seen*". (Heb. 1:1) The very nature of the verse begs the challenge of testing and perseverance.

It was the late seventies, I had left a lucrative secular position and answered God's call on our life to full time Christian service. Monetarily it was quite challenging. Where once, meeting all our needs was not so burdensome; now our resolve was tested. During this time my wife, Lana, was put to the test of faithfully discharging her role for our family of six. If keeping up with the washing in a home with four active children wasn't enough of a strain, imagine accomplishing the task with a washing machine that lacked in operating up to par – it would wash but not rinse the clothes.

Funds to purchase a major appliance were scarce, and even though we could have borrowed enough to cover the acquisition, that wouldn't require faith. Because of her prayers, she believed God would provide. So, every wash day she praised the Lord that the clothes came out clean, and resolutely extracted the water by forcibly wringing every piece of garment. We know that God could have blessed us with a miraculous gift at the outset, but He allowed her endurance to be tested. How long would it be before she would cry out "How long O Lord?" Or arrive at the place where she would concede and say, "Let's just go buy one?"

I don't remember how long she was asked to wait, but one fateful day a friend called asking us to come over because he had something to give us. You can guess what it was – a washer. No, it wasn't new, but did perform perfectly; plus, there was a dryer that matched the very popular avocado colored washer of the day. In addition, a much-needed clothes dresser the kids were desperate for; rounding out the items prayed over. I submit, the Lord 'walked' beside her until they 'got into the boat'. Her '*hope*' was focused on the '*assurance*' promised by our Lord; and convinced that whatever the span of time; by faith would see the '*things not seen.*'

The writer continues his exhortation on faith by drawing attention to the fact that "*by it the men of old gained approval.*" True heroes! Unwavering in their devotion to the One who is unwavering in His promises. These 'characterizations' of faith are, in part, designed to refocus our attention on the reality that these examples of trustworthy behavior elevate their status to being genuine heroes. I emphasize this to accent the fact that many referred to as the, so-called, heroes of today do not come close to measuring up to those we will peruse. Can we put into question those in Athletics? Or Hollywood? Or the Music Field? Or Politics? Or even some in the Pastorate? I think not!

Next, the scribe takes us to the beginning. "*By faith we understand that the worlds were prepared by the word of God, so that what was seen was not made out of things which are visible.*" One is intrigued by the number of times we are taken back to creation – the foundation of faith. It wasn't as if God made visible what was formerly invisible; He spoke the heavens and the earth into existence from nothing. The fundamentals of our faith are rooted in the fact of God's Creation. "*Then God said, 'Let there be light; and there was light.*'" (Gen.1:3)

Let me say again, 'our faith is rooted in the fact of God's creation.' When one is fully persuaded that 'out of nothing' comes the beauty and wonder of all that God '*spoke*' into existence; a life of confidence and conviction will manifest itself, and infect, their being.

But, in today's culture, creation is, not only, called into question, but is an offense to, and calls into question the very nature of who God is. In the Book of Mark, chapter 10, Jesus was confronted by some Pharisees who desired to test Him concerning divorce. They made their case by quoting that "*Moses permitted a man to write a certificate of divorce and send her away.*" (Mk.10:4). Jesus responded by noting it was because of "*the hardness of heart He*" did so. Then Jesus challenged their thinking by stating, "*from the beginning of creation, God made them male and female.... the two shall become one flesh....what God joined together, let no man separate.*" (Mk.10:6-9)

We see our present culture challenging God's very nature, which is brought into question because of the way many believe truth is not dictated on God's immutable word – but truth is founded upon the direction that the culture is going.

For the Pharisees:

Their emphasis was the present-day culture.

For Jesus:

the emphasis was upon the beginning –
Divinity in creation.

Almost every decision promoted in this country today challenges and assaults God's Creation.

Abortion: God is the creator of every life – no matter the circumstances. He controls the womb. All born are under His authority and not to be exterminated. Ps. 139:13-16; Jer.1:5

Trans-gender; Gay: God created 'male and female'. That marks the essence of every relationship entered into. Gender is determined solely by The Creator, not by human emotions or yearnings, or operations. Rom.1:21-32; 1 Cor. 6:9.10

Critical Race Theory; Black Lives Matter; Equity: Equity no! Equality, yes! (Proved by the Trinity – Jn. 14: 23; Matt.13:19; 2 Cor.13:14). Every life matters because every life is created by God. He decided how genealogies would formulate and how continents would congregate before the foundation of the world. Gen. 11:6-9; Omniscience (all-knowing) John 1:48

*Note concerning 'Equity': No doubt you are aware of the "Great Reset." The basics contain the goal to establish 'fairness.' The primary question: how this is achieved! The answer. Lower the status, expectations, and function presently in force to make it easier for everyone to accomplish the prize. How might this affect "religion?" The Bible is no longer the supreme authority. When it states, "*for there is no other name (Jesus Christ) under heaven that has been given...by which we must be saved.*" (Acts 4:12) *Jesus is the only way*! Religion will eradicate this absolute and include any and every teaching.

Cancel Cultural: Every aspect of life is in the hands of the creator. The value of their birth; their life; and their death. It's called: Omnipotence (all-powerful) Matt. 28:18)

I submit that John puts an emphasis on the Creator in the first few verses of his Gospel. He leads off his dissertation (chapter 1) by verifying the Person in reference is declared to be.

God incarnate. "*In the beginning was the Word, and the Word was with God, and the* *Word (Jesus) was God*. *He was in the beginning with God.*" (*vs.*1,2) Once John establishes who God, The Son is, he authenticates His role in creation by stating: "*All things came into being by Him, and apart from Him nothing came into being that has come into being*" (vs.3). It was then he added, "*In Him is life. And life is the light of men.*" (vs.4)

In this Order:

1. ***Jesus is Fully God.***

2. ***Jesus is The Creator.***

3. ***Jesus is the life giver.***

So, I conclude, when I came to Christ by grace through faith alone (Eph.2:8,9 – Justification), I "accepted" and "*received*" Him (Jn.1:11,12) as "*God and Savior*" (Tit.2:13), Redeemer (Eph.1:7), Lord (Mt.22:43-45), "*The King of kings and Lord of lords*" (*Rev.*19:16), "*The Light of the world*" (*Jn.*8:12). It's little wonder, then, that I would accept Him as The Creator of the world and live like it. All Is sanctioned as fact and is never ascribed to question. Therefore, His Words (Scriptures) are without error; factual in every way (2 Tim.3:16,17). Consequently, in whatever direction the culture precedes, it will never alter the word of God – the Word of God is to always alter the culture. By rejecting the above – I would be rejecting Him.

We have an example back in the 'beginning': The "*serpent was more crafty than any other beast*" (Gen.3:1-7). He approached Eve saying, "*Indeed, has God said, 'You shall not eat from any tree in the garden'*? Eve responded, "*From the fruit of the trees of the garden we may eat; but from the fruit of the tree in the middle of the garden. God has said, 'You shall not eat from it or touch it, lest you die.'*" (An example of living by faith). The 'serpent', the devil, wanted her to live by sight and stated, "*You surely shall not die.... God knows when you eat.... your eyes will be opened, and you will be like God.*" Eve's eyes were "opened;" She "*saw that the tree was good for food.....it was a delight to the eyes.....it was desirable to make one wise.*" In a matter of moments, Eve left a heavenly place (living by faith) to accept living in a lowly way (living by sight).

Our life in Christ begins in such a way; every path our Lord leads us into will hold opportunities to live by faith and not by sight. Our response should remain in accordance with

His will and walk in glorious and victorious faith. Knowing Him so intimately will secure "*the things hoped for, and conviction of things not seen*".

Even though I might prefer to be carried by my Lord through the difficult times, I'm convinced the level of faith that I grow in will be increased because of His choice in allowing me to walk beside Him – with His hand on my shoulder. Our study through Hebrews 11 will allow us to examine this truth.

My Personal "Faith Walk" Journal – Ch.1

(Meditate and respond to the following questions)

1. What current storm in your life is causing you to fall; to doubt God's promises; and/or to lose your faith as you take your eyes off Jesus in the midst of the storm?

____

____

____

____

2. How do you find peace and keep your faith amid the storms in your life?

____

____

____

____

3. God uses tests in our life to grow and mature us in our faith (James 1: 2-4). Take a moment to remember a time or times in your past in which God faithfully brought you through a very difficult time, and in the process grew your faith and trust in Him.

Who can you share this with to encourage in their trial, as well as encourage yourself in your own faith walk by this memory.

4. In what ways does knowing and believing that God created this world we live in, out of absolutely nothing, enhance your faith?

5. We certainly live in a world and culture today that has become more and more anti-God, and more and more hostile toward those with strong Biblical views.

____

____

____

____

Do you find it easier to ignore, and not get involved, in what those pushing anti Biblical agendas are doing?

____

____

Or do you seek to take a strong stand for the Truth of Scripture in this present day, even though you come up against many who are in opposition to what you believe? Even those who are close.

____

____

____

6. On a scale from 1 to ten, with 1 being "fully walking by sight" and 10 being "fully walking and living by faith", how would you rate your faith walk at this point of your life?

____

____

____

____

Growing in faith is a process – What can/will you do to take your faith walk to the next level?

____

____

CHAPTER TWO

Heb. 11: 4

" Faith Humbles Itself Under God's Authority "

"By faith Abel offered to God a better sacrifice than Cain, through which he obtained the testimony that he was righteous, God testifying about his gifts, and through faith, though he is dead, he still speaks."

Heb. 11: 4

The first example the scribe of Hebrews pens is that of the tragic account of murder early in the history of man. We are befuddled as to how such a grievous act could take place so early at the onset of time. The only plausible answer is that the 'serpent' who prompted Eve to sin was the same 'serpent' who was "*crouching at the door*" (*Gen*.4:7) of Cain's heart enticing his rebellion.

If we are transported back to that event endeavoring to gain some insight into how it all transpired, Genesis 4 is our text. We have two brothers; only two boys who, apparently, were challenged to present their offerings before the Lord. Cain the older, "*was a tiller of the ground*" (*vs*.2); and Abel the younger, "*was a keeper of flocks*" (vs.2). Every indication we are given in the passage suggests their sincerity in what they were willing to give.

"*Cain brought an offering to the Lord of the fruit of the ground*" (*vs*3). *Abel brought off the firstlings of his flock and of their fat portions*" (*vs*.4). The scriptures go on to relate that "*the Lord had regard for Abel and his offering; but for Cain and for his offering had no regard*". (vs. 4,5) Consequently, Cain became very "*angry*", and his "*countenance*" fell.

God confronted Cain by quizzing him concerning his anger. "W*hy are you angry? If you do well, will not your countenance be lifted up*? Then our Lord warned Cain, "*If you do not do well, sin is crouching at the door; and its desire is for you, but you must master it*". (vs. 7)

This is illustrated in 1 Peter 5:8. He writes, "*Your adversary, the devil (serpent) prowls about like a roaring lion, seeking someone to devour*?" What was the fundamental conundrum? Cain needed to "*humble himself*" (1Pet.5:6). Here-in lies the heart of our lesson.

Before we continue, let me offer to you a suggestion to answer the often-asked question: 'Why didn't God accept Cain's offering? After all, God had made provision for "grain" offerings to be brought". (Lev.2:1,4,14,15) I offer this for your consideration.

When Adam and Eve ate from the forbidden tree, in the garden of Eden, they "*hid themselves from the presence of the Lord*" for "*they knew they were naked; and sewed fig leaves together and made themselves loin coverings*". (Gen. 3:7,8) The "*Lord came in the cool of the day*" (Gen3:8) wanting to fellowship with His created beings but found them hiding. Why were they in concealment? Weren't they 'covered'? Weren't their actions sufficient? Of course not! Only God's initiating actions can bring about restoration. Adam and Eve's answer characterized works – living by sight. God's answer would symbolize grace – living by faith. Therefore, there was only one remedy for this dilemma, The "*Lord God made garments of skin for Adam and his wife and clothed them*". (Gen.3:21) Blood was spilt for the reconciliation of man. A means that would be in effect throughout man's time on earth. <u>Abel got it! Cain didn't!</u> Abel's gift to the Lord represented an act of grace – 'faith'. Cain's offering an act of <u>his works</u> – 'sight'.

When Peter spoke of the "adversary" (the devil) wanting to "devour" any unwary soul; he links a defense against the ***"roaring lion"*** - very simply put -

"<u>*Humble yourself*</u>" - *Mostly*; this is easier said than done!

The penman of Hebrews begins his list of exemplifications on faith where he confronts us with our primary battle ground - Pride - Arrogance - exercising self-will over God's will. The scene of Abel bringing his offering representing the "*firstlings of his flock and of their fat portions*" (Gen.4:4) to the Lord. In my spirit I see him bowing in reverence and praise, worshiping with a whole heart. It's no wonder why God "*had regard for Abel and his offering*". Abel's gift originated from "*fear (reverence) of the Lord*", understanding "*before honor comes humility*". (Prov.15:33)

What a victory over the 'adversary' when "*those who (humbly) wait for the Lord*" and "*gain new strength.*" (Isa.40:31) It signifies the elevation of putting God's will ahead of our uncontrollable will. <u>Pride will simply not allow for the patience it takes while God is working His miracle in a life. Vanity has an insatiable appetite for recognition</u>. It says, 'I want acknowledgement - and I want it now!' Peter stated, "*Humble yourself under the mighty hand of God, that he may exalt you at the proper time*". (1 Pet.5:6)

Our first example of faith, Abel, fits all the criteria of one 'living by faith and not sight. We are told Abel brought the 'firstlings' as his proposal to God. This expresses the submission of that which he considers of highest priority in his life. The 'first-fruit'! This begs a question for us. ((When it's time to write our tithe check to the Lord, do we write it out 'first' – based on the total amount of finances, or compose the check, 'last', on what is left over. Of course, it's taking more faith to frame it first). Also, Abel didn't hold any of his offering back, for "*their fat portion*" was presented. Of course, it requires more faith to not hold anything back.

Allow me to also offer this thought: Cain related to his brother his plight (Gen.4:8). And next a confrontation is brought to our attention where "*Cain rose up against Abel, his brother and killed him.*" My quandary arises from the fact that "*they were in the field.*" Why did Abel go out to the field? My take? Due to his character of possessing a humble spirit, he would approach his brother endeavoring to encourage him. To have him make his heart right in the sight of the Lord God.

It requires abundant faith to move toward our enemies while seeking to make things right.

Cain is at a crossroad! What he does next will speak of his character! God "*had no regard*" for his offering. His little brother's offering was 'regarded" but not the eldest; the one to whom should have been an example to the younger now suffers rejection from the Lord. Who wants rejection? Who wants to deal with rejection? Most often, anger will ensue.

It definitely riled Cain who demonstrated indignation to the max. Remember! He became "*very angry and his countenance fell. The Lord said to Cain, 'Why are you angry?*

And why has your countenance fallen? If you do well, will not your countenance be lifted? And if you do not do well....'" (Gen.4:5-7) Herein is found the foundation of the problem – the nitty-gritty as it were. The 'battle ground'! If we are honest, we all are quite familiar with this predicament. We are fully aware of what we should do before the Lord – but something (someone?) clouds our resolve, and we rebel against what is <u>just</u> to carry out what is <u>unjust</u>.

Cain chose the latter and experienced "*sin crouching at the door....it desires you*". The very "*devil...who prowls about like a roaring lion*", that Peter refers to. God continued his reproof by stating, "*You must master it*". It was with Cain, as it can, also. Be with us. A humble heart would choose to "do well" – pride will choose to be stiff-necked.

Pride; Arrogance; Pomp; Haughtiness; Ostentatious: Whatever name is associated to describe it – it is sin. Lucifer is a prime example as pictured by Isaiah; chapter 14: 11-14.

Humility submits itself to the will of God – pride exercises its own will. Satan propounded his rebellious attitude by declaring what he was going to do: "*I will!*" Not once, twice, or three times, but five times this arrogant angel; the "*anointed cherub*" (Ezek.28:14); boasted of how he would rise above the True and Living God. Hearing himself make such a claim must have made him feel he was at the apex of his lifc. But God didn't allow for this feeling to persist very long, God made his own declaration: "*you will be thrust down to Sheol*" (Isa.14:15). Solomon, the wisest man who ever lived, wrote; "*Pride goes before destruction, and a haughty spirit before stumbling*" (Prov.16:18).

> There's one thing about egotism: Truth of who we are can hit us in the face but will not believe we have been affected in any way. Others maybe, but it won't touch us. Sadly though, it will every time

I wish I could say, "I'm clueless about such things." But I can't! As He was with Cain, God is willing to patiently work with us as well.

We had been in full time Christian service for a few years serving as associate pastor in Central California. Anointing was upon the church there; we saw wonderful growth in every way. One day an opportunity came our way to serve as Pastor in a church near Sacramento; sensing God's hand in it, we accepted the call to go.

I was aware that this church had a history of being a challenging ministry. Others had endeavored to strengthen the work, but to no avail. Why would I be inclined to undertake such a summons? Because I said to myself: "*I will*" make it work. I'm not sure if I said "I will" five times but the same arrogance prompted my thoughts as it had Lucifer. For two years there was one attempt after another to build a thriving ministry, but every amount of effort came up empty. God had sent us there all right, not to build a church, but to allow me to "fail."

The Lord removed us from that body of believers and out of the pastorate for the next three years. In Christian service, yes, but feeling like I had been shelved. Again, not a total loss, but not realizing the fullness of what I sensed my call was. Five not so joyous years, but five necessary years of being trained by the best in His field. This training is designed to prepare us for future opportunities to be used by the Lord in a productive way. It is so important to understand God's love for us moves Him to discipline us for our own good and for His ultimate good.

Some hints for 'humbling ourselves' includes: 1. "*Seek first the Kingdom of God*". (Mt. 6:25-34) 2. "*Put on the full armor of God.*" (Eph. 6:10-18) 3. Have Christ's attitude. (Phil. 2:5-11) 4. Maintain a heart for prayer. (Col. 4:2) 5. Make truth an absolute necessity. (John 8: 31.32)

Abel, the first offspring used to illustrate faith, demonstrates the importance of possessing a humble heart before the Lord; always aware of His will; and diligent to honor it. Not desiring any exaltation now but looking for the day that God will honor him. (1 Pet. 5:6)

My Personal "Faith Walk" Journal – Ch. 2

1. While Satan, the serpent, is not all-knowing (Omniscient) as God is, he is very aware of our individual weaknesses; and he, also his demonic forces, are ever waiting for an opportune time to attack us. * If you have questions concerning his activities – please contact me – kingdomliving17@yahoo.com

____

____

____

____

What sin or sins are crouching at your heart's door?

____

____

2. How can you know that the offering you are planning to give to the Lord will be acceptable and pleasing to Him?

____

____

____

____

____

3. Just as God confronted Cain regarding his anger, so God confronts us in regard to our sins:

    a. Through conviction by the Holy Spirit (John 16: 8);

____

    b. Through conviction via God's Word (2 Tim. 3: 16);

____

    c. Also, conviction by our own conscience (John 8: 8) As well as others.

____

Is God confronting you now of any unconfessed sin in your life?

____

____

4. Sometimes God does allow us to "fail" in order to teach us, correct us and grow us in our faith, so he can mold us into the likeness of His Son, Jesus. No one wants or likes to fail, however, if God chooses to bring a failure in your life – according to His plan – and according to His purpose:

____

____

____

____

____

How would you respond?

____

____

5. It has been stated: "Pride is a passion that perpetuates anger, hurt, and foolishness while keeping at bay the restorative effects of conviction, humility, and reconciliation."

____

____

____

____

____

How do you respond to this truth?

____

____

There is no question that most people, including Christians, struggle at times with the sin of "pride." How does a person break free from the chains and bondage of pride to a freedom of humility?

____

____

____

6. Jesus is the perfect example of what true humility look like; and He demonstrates that humility in many, many ways – especially in His death on calvary's cross for all who believe.

____

____

____

____

What are some practical ways you can demonstrate humility to those:

a. In your family?

____

b. Who is in your workplace?

____

c. Who is in your church family?

____

d. In your immediate neighborhood?

____

CHAPTER THREE

Heb. 11:5,6

" Ultimate Faith Prompts God to Expand the Ordinary "

"By faith Enoch was taken up so he should not see death; And he was not found because God took him up; for he obtained the witness that before his being taken up, he was pleasing to God. And without faith it is impossible to please Him, for he who comes to God must believe that He is, and that he is a rewarder of those who seek Him.

Heb.11:5,6

In chapter 9 of Hebrews verse 27, it states, "*Inasmuch as it is appointed for men to die* <u>*once*</u> *and after this comes judgment.*" If this biblical principle is in force from Genesis to Revelation, why an exception here? Intriguing question! More intriguing contemplation! Why would God lay aside a teaching that represents a 'rule of thumb' for humanity? Because of the incredible faith of Enoch! <u>An extraordinary faith will produce extraordinary results</u>.

As I recall an event from my childhood, I'm reminded of an occurrence my family experienced when I was about 8 years old - 1950. My dad, who was a wonderful standard bearer of faith, was Pastoring in Washington State. His and my mom's family resided in Minnesota. Every two years they would have family reunions, which we had been to before. This particular year, 1950, for some reason, my dad had a longing to drive the, almost, 1500 miles to attend this kinfolk event. Problem? No finances!

Dad was not one to dwell on the obvious, but on the possibilities of what God can do. So, he exhorted us to get ready to go. My practical mom would, slightly, counter with, "Ray, let's not get the kids all worked up. What if it doesn't happen?" "I believe the Lord would have us attend." Dad gently insisted. Sound familiar? Ever happen to you?

Then one day, at dinner time, we were all gathered around the table enjoying the cuisine my mom had prepared.

Suddenly, we heard a noise coming from the front door. It was kind of familiar, but not that easily detectable. We all rushed to discover the mystery and found a cute little puppy pompously sitting on the steps with a paper bag in its mouth. "What in the world is this"? Everyone wondered: then Dad reached down securing the paper bag; opened it and found it full of money. We all scurried into the kitchen to count out the cash - $200.00.

Interesting! What happened to the puppy? Don't know! I always believed it was an angel.

One might think $200.00 isn't very much until one realizes that costs were much different in 1950. For instance: New Ford= $1300.00; Gas= .20 cents a gal.; Bread=.14 cents a loaf; Potatoes= .35 cents@ 5 lbs.; Sugar= .43 cents @5 lbs. Milk= .80 @gal

Dad took the money down to the police station where he was told they would keep it for a week, and if no one claimed the windfall, it would be his. A week went by – no one affirmed a loss – it was given to us. Shortly after, we headed east to reunite with our relatives. God had moved in a unique way because He had witnessed exceptional faith. This would be the last time my parents would see their parents alive.

Extraordinary Faith Produces Extraordinary Results!

The question is how do we measure up? Here's an interesting proposition. Jesus said:

> "***Truly I say to you, whoever says to this mountain, 'Be taken up and cast into the sea,' and does not doubt in his heart, but believes that what he says is going to happen, it shall be granted him. Therefore, I say to you, all things for which you pray and ask, believe you have received them, and they shall be granted you,***"
>
> (Mk. 11: 23,24)

Do we really believe this extraordinary exhortation? Or do we tend to explain away the literalness of this verse. I'm afraid the latter is generally true. So, Jesus lied? Can't say that! Then He was just kidding; He knew it wasn't possible; it was just an illustration to get the people thinking. I submit that Jesus does not lie, nor does He just kid around to be controversial. <u>He means what He says- and says what He means!</u> Our conundrum is a weakness in our faith. Our ability to 'see' the 'unseen' is clouded by our practical flesh. Thus, the tendency is to disregard the teaching and miss out on a potential miracle.

Enoch did not suffer from such an ailment. He possessed a passion for wanting to 'please' God, for it is impossible to please our Lord void of faith. This is clarified in the list of Patriarchs in Genesis 5, the woeful entries listed, ended as such. With each registration: 1. The name was given. 2. The age when becoming a father. 3. The length of years lived after that birth. 4. The age "*when he died.*" Every account proclaimed the words, "*when he died*" – with one exception – Enoch (Gen.5:21-24). Again, a life out of the ordinary.

There is so little recorded of his life, and so much more we yearn to know. It causes a search to glean every tidbit of truth to be digested into our soul. Drawn back into Hebrews 11, attention is given to verse 6. "***For he who comes to God must believe that He is,***"

I offer the following for your consideration. By reflecting on the previous verse, and the appending of Jude 14, 15, Enoch seemed to grasp truths cognizant by he alone with this prophecy.

"***Behold the Lord came with many thousands of His holy ones, to execute judgment upon all, and to convict all the ungodly of all their ungodly deeds which they have done in an ungodly way, and all the harsh things which ungodly sinners have spoken against Him.***"

Teaching attributed to The Lord Jesus mounted upon a "white horse" coming back at the second coming "*waging war*" on sin. And "*armies in heaven*" following on "*white horses*" (Rev.19:11-14) prompts our attention to the fact that Enoch comprehended data that can only be given through the anointing of the Holy Spirit. Imagine, Enoch, having a clear perception of the Person of the Lord Jesus Christ, and the means of Salvation.

"And without 'faith' it is impossible to please Him, for he who comes to God must 'believe' that He is, and He is the rewarder of those who seek Him." (Heb.11:6,7)

Envision a man living 3400 BC being 'rewarded' for his desire to "seek Him". Feasting on the manna of reconciliation by grace through faith that would materialize years later. Isn't this the fruit of '*walking with God?*" When you walk – you talk. Enoch "walked with God' for 365 years. They walked and talked – talked and walked, until one day they walked into heaven with our Lord's hand upon his shoulder. In this way he was found to be "pleasing" to the Lord and the recipient of an unusual, and powerful blessing. <u>He was taken!</u>

As I sit here writing of such events in biblical history – I long to be more knowledgeable in reference to Enoch – sorry, I'm not able – but this I know:

"Extraordinary Faith Produces Extraordinary Results"

A question for each of us: "How can I know I will be taken to heaven?"

"*And the witness is this, that God has given eternal life , and this life is in His Son. He who has the Son has the life; he who does not have the Son of God does not have the life*". *These things I have written to you who believe in the name of the Son of God, in order that you may know you have eternal life*". (1 Jn.5;11-13) You can actually be certain, confident, and assured that you will possess heaven. Meditate on the following – asking the Holy Spirit to reveal His truth.

1. "*For all have sinned and fallen short of the glory of God*". (Rom. 3: 23)
2. "*For the wages of sin is death, but the free gift of God is eternal life in Jesus Christ our Lord*". (Rom.6:23)
3. "*But God demonstrated His own love toward us, in that while we were yet sinners, Christ died for us*". (Rom.5:8)
4. "*If you confess with your mouth Jesus as Lord and believe in your heart that God raised Him from the dead, you shall be saved; for with the heart man believes, resulting in*

*righteousness, and with the mouth he confesses, resulting in salvation...**for whoever will call upon the name of the Lord will be saved".*** (Rom.10:9,10,13)

5. In prayer, ask the Lord to come into your life and forgive your sins - purpose before Him to be willing to change whatever He deems necessary to reflect His power and grace in your life.

* Now contact someone you know to be a Christian - tell them about your decision to follow Christ as your Savior. You can also contact me - kingdomliving17@yahoo.com

My Personal "Faith Walk" Journal: Ch. 3

---

1. When it comes to passages of scripture as we examined in Mark 11, where Jesus posed a challenge of what can take place when one prays in faith. Really? Mountains can be moved!

How do you respond to these and other similar teachings; Ignore? Explain away? Or believe!

____

____

2. What example comes to your mind from your life experience in which an extraordinary faith produced an extraordinary result?

____

____

How did that situation encourage you in your faith then?

____

____

How is it continuing to encourage you in your faith now?

____

____

3. What potential miracles have you missed out on because of:

____

____

Doubt?

____

____

Weakness of faith?

____

____

4. While we are not told a lot about Enoch in the Bible, we still can learn from him, because of his great faith, and how he lived his life. What does God want you to learn and put into practice?

5. The most important decision in life that each of us must make concerns Christ. In that decision, we either accept Christ as Savior, or we reject Him. This decision determines where we will spend Eternity.

If you should die tonight; do you know with full assurance where you will spend Eternity?

If you have doubt, please contact me –
kingdomliving17@yahoo.com

6. Satan, the father of lies and great deceiver, will attack believers, at times, with lies and false accusations to create doubt of true salvation; therefore, weakening their faith. Salvation is a gift from the Lord God through the work of Jesus Christ – His gift is based on security.

Look up the following Scriptures and respond to each.

John 10: 27-30:

____

____

1 John 5: 11 – 13:

____

____

When Jesus was tempted by Satan in the wilderness (Matt.4: 1-11) , He used Scripture to counter Satan's attacks – study the Scriptures (like the above) so you, also, can counter the attacks.

CHAPTER FOUR

Heb. 11: 7

" Faith That Willingly Stands Alone "

"By faith Noah being warned by God about things not yet seen, in reverence prepared an ark for the salvation of his household. By which he condemned the world and became an heir of the righteousness which is according to faith."

(Heb. 11: 7)

The understatement of all time! "*Noah found favor in the eyes of the Lord.*" (Gen.6:8) This utterance on the heels of God saying that He "*was sorry He made man on the earth.*" (Gen.6:6) If that had come to pass, I wouldn't be exhausting you right now and you wouldn't be exhausted – <u>we wouldn't be</u>! I'm so thrilled with Noah - I will have to tell him so someday.

What would bring God to the point of speaking such futility? Disobedient angels who had fallen with Lucifer! Not fully understanding the impact of this reality where "*sons of God saw that the daughters of men were beautiful and took wives for themselves, - they came into the daughters of men, and they bore children to them – Nephilim – mighty men – men of renown.*" (Gen.6:1-5)

The essence of creation was tainted, God's design for humanity thwarted by self- seeking demons desirous of creating their own "I will" race. The sight caused God to be "*grieved in His heart*" *and said,* "*I will blot out man whom I have created from the face of the land, from man to animals to creeping things and to birds of the sky; for I am sorry I have made them.*'" (Gen.6:6,7) Thus the call on Noah, a man to whom God "*favored*", a man Peter would refer to as a "*preacher of righteousness*" (2 Pet.2:5). A man who would stand alone against adversity because he "*was blameless in his time*" – his faith would surely be tested.

"*Make for yourself an ark!*" (Gen.6:14) "What's an ark?" God had taken great pains in giving exact details for the craft to be built. The dimensions. The decks. The materials. The animals and birds, how clean and unclean. Right down to the placement of the sole window, and the door. What to take and what not to take. Every detail encased for this floating sanctuary that would sustain his family from any peril.

All these instructions were consigned with authority and anointing because they were the very Word of God. "*And Noah did according to all that the Lord had commanded him.*" (Gen.7:5) Noah had been "*warned by God of things yet not seen.*" (*Heb.*11:7) The passage continues its insight by stating, "*in reverence (he) prepared an ark for the salvation of his household.*" The very nature of his activities would condemn the world.

With the project completed, God confirmed by stating, "I *will send rain*" (Gen.7:4) "What's rain?"

No doubt, the condemned world, who could not comprehend the unseen, attacked Noah and his sons every move. The Patriarch must have had thick skin to repel the onslaught of vicious insults from the profane. I'm curious though, how did the boy's resolve hold up? Did they voice, "Another fine mess you've gotten us into again, dad!" Perhaps!

Truth is Dad, Mom, Grandparents; it's, not only, our faith that produces a steadfast purpose for us, but serves as an influence for our household – those who might have a weaker faith. When the hostilities bear down upon us, our faith raises the confidence of all around us. So, let the ignorant come and shout their disparaging remarks like:

"WHAT'S AN ARK?" or "WHAT'S RAIN?" or "STUPID IS WHAT STUPID DOES"

How does one cope with and endure through all the Rederick cast by the ignorance of the world? Faith! And where does faith originate from? The Word of God! This prompts one to return to some of the fundamentals of Scriptural truth concerning faith.

1. *Without faith it is impossible to please Him* (God). (Heb.11:6)
2. "*Faith comes by hearing, and hearing by the word of Christ* (God). (Rom.10:17)
3. "*You are protected by the power of God through faith*". (I Pet.1:5)
4. "*...and the stability of your faith in Christ*". (Col. 2:5)
5. *Trials*: "*The testing of our faith produces endurance.*" (Jms.1:2-4)

I submit that Noah could remain steadfast in the decree given by God to finish the titanic task and endured through all the disparaging comments from the enemy because he believed in and trusted The Word of God. He had "*taken up the shield of faith and extinguished the flaming missiles of the evil one.*" (Eph.6:16) As we have seen in Hebrews 11, faith is grounded. in "*assurance*" and "*conviction.*" With the number of postering's we face in our culture almost daily that requires some level of response; living by faith is not an option if our desire is to duplicate Noah's fortitude. Noah was victorious due to his ability to humbly accept God's word as absolute and follow its directives to the letter.

Question is: To Whom do we go to find the same tenacity for faithfulness? A voice on the internet? The loudest voice of the day? The richest voice of the day? The voice of the one who has the largest church? The Whom we are to seek first is the One who saved our soul, the One who represents the very foundation of our faith.

It is extremely possible that we might face an onslaught of disparaging commentary if God tarries in His return for His Bride. We live in a world fraught with danger. Many in high places endeavor to inflict us with fear, with a motive to control. Every day the airwaves – are filled with news that can potentially alter our very earthly existence. (Praise God, it can't alter our heavenly existence.)

The commitments we make now, prior to the demonic aggression, will determine how we fare through till the end. The foundations fashioned upon the Word of God now will ascertain how herculean the strength of the structure built in the name of the Lord. Endure or fall?

Remain true or apostate? Remain fearless or shrink-back? Only in the Scriptures do we find 'Words' that, 'protect by power' – enjoy 'stability' – and 'endurance'.

A few paragraphs back, I shared a curious musing; "did the boys (Ham, Shem, and Japheth) maintain their resolve?" The level of robust faith found in God's servants often will depend on the level of robust faith found in their closest confidants. It can be a two-way avenue of stimulating one another. I'm persuaded it to be a family affair. If Noah was feeling low, the others would lift him up. If the family suffered from mental exhaustion, Noah bolstered their faith. If all were travailing in skepticism, perhaps Enoch's son Methuselah, who had faith mentored to him, would intervene on their behalf to stimulate unwavering trust In God and press on to victory.

I recall a particular incident experienced by our family back in 1977. As I mentioned previously, the Lord moved us from secular work into the ministry. This was a time where many adjustments of sacrifice would be made. Adjusting to a new neighborhood - adjusting to new acquaintances – adjusting to a lower income – adjusting to new routines – adjusting to those who would scrutinize the decision. On every level, every family member was required to modify their life – defiantly a step of faith for each. (Except maybe Amy, she was a newborn, business as usual for her, no reason to be concerned).

For dad, this was a solemn moment of contemplation! Was the family on board? Was this just my hair-brained idea? Actually, Lana and I were of the same mindset that God had orchestrated the events, but what about the kids?

One specific day I picked up our twelve-year-old daughter Lindy from school. So, I thought this would be as good a time as any to inquire; "How do you feel about the prospect of moving to a new town"? As I recall, she hesitated a moment – I guessed it was because she would be leaving her BFF – looking down, very simply, she said, "Whatever you think is right is ok with me." That became the general consensus of every family member and faith was increased because of the elemental dialogue.

I believe God's call upon the life of Noah, as ours, was a family affair. They would serve in one accord. Trusting in one another – encouraging one another – fortifying one another. God's hand resting upon the shoulders of His chosen ministers. Finding relief only when it was time to enter the Ark – God's temporal sanctuary for them to experience His sovereignty.

The day came when they could look back on the ordeal and with thanksgiving "*Noah built an alter to the Lord,*" God "*smelled the soothing aroma,*" (Gen.8:20,21) and was so pleased a new covenant was established. Make no mistake, our faith pleases our God.

Since I lean toward the actions of Noah representing a banner example of walking by faith, I must bring out a prevailing principle that can take place on the heels of such action.

What a tragedy that only some seventy-five to one hundred years later we have a grievous situation like the 'Tower of Babel'. Considering the apparent level of spirituality, of the eight who debarked the Ark; we ask, how could they spiral out of control - desiring to be like God in such a short period of time. This was Noah's own family, sons and grandsons. God had to intervene and alter His creation which would affect every human thereafter.

Similar circumstances can affect our personal lives. Victories one day – defeats the next. These plights present our need to keep looking to "*Jesus, the author and perfecter of faith*". (Heb.12:2) – praying for those close to us; and discipling those in our sphere of influence.

My Personal "Walk of Faith" Journal: Ch. 4

1. "*Noah found favor in the eyes of the Lord.*" God makes this powerful statement – then uses Noah in a powerful way. What would it mean in your life for God "*to find favor*" in you?

Would it alter your thinking and/or actions?

2. If you, as Noah was, asked by God to face a situation where you must take a stand for a Biblical principle – and instructed go alone – going against a very hostile people/person – whose beliefs are in opposition to yours. What would you do?

____

____

What kind of courage does this take?

____

____

3. A strong faith in us can, and will, influence others to walk by faith. When we stand strong for Truth, others will be encouraged to stand also.

____

____

Are you influencing anyone in your sphere of influence?

____

____

Are people interested in Christ's salvation because of your influence?

____

____

4. Spending a consistent and regular exercise in God's Word equates with being "found in favor" with our Lord. Bible study is essential for personal growth and spiritual maturity. Noah obediently listened too and followed each instruction given by the Lord God. This represents asking:

____

____

   a. Do you read God's Word? What's your involvement?

____

____

   b. Do you meditate on God's Word?

____

____

c. Do you feel you hear and heed its instruction?

____

____

d. Are you aware of how it is increasing your faith?

____

____

5. Someone in your sphere of influence needs the encouragement and support you have to give. As you apply the principles you've been introduced to in this study, you will grow in faith.

____

____

Bow before the Lord inquiring who He would have you encourage and support – thus building them up in the faith.

____

____

CHAPTER FIVE

Heb. 11: 8 - 10

" Abraham's Life Reveals How One Grows in Faith "

Abraham, when he was called, obeyed by going out to a place which he was to receive for an inheritance; and he went out, not where he was going. By faith he lived as an alien in the land of promise, as in a foreign land, dwelling in tents with Isaac and Jacob, fellow heirs of the same promise; for he was looking for the city which has foundations, whose architect and builder is God."

(Heb.11:8-10)

There is no way we can conclude what Abram was involved in when he heard God's call on his life. Living in Ur of the Chaldeans, his life might have been filled with opportunities of agriculture for Mesopotamia was nestled between the Tigris and Euphrates rivers (present day Iraq). Fertile lands abounded for the growing of sustainable crops and herds of sheep and goats. Then one day, "*The God of glory appeared to Abraham" and said, "Depart from your country and your relatives, and come to the land that I will show you.*" (Acts 7:2-4)

A question one might ask is, "How did Abram know who God was?" We are given a hint from Luke's (3:34-36) genealogy of Jesus. He declares that Abram was a grandson of Seth, Noah's son. We learn that Seth was 425 years old when Abram was born and, interestingly enough, died about the same time; Seth was 600 years old and Abraham 175 around 2000 bc.

What's the point? There is no reason not to think that Shem and Abram hung out together in Mesopotamia. I can see them sitting around the campfire by night listening to the history of God's creation up to the flood, the tower of Babel, and the dispersion of man upon the earth; all which Shem witnessed. Imagine! No media, no devices; just quality time spent face to face, actually communicating orally the wonders of the Most High God.

The day comes when God invokes His will upon Abram to follow His decree as given in Acts 7, that we quoted above. Yet we read in Gen. 11:31 that "*Tarah took Abram his son, Lot...his grandson, and Sari his daughter-in-law...and they went out together from Ur of the Chaldeans in order to enter the land of Canaan.*"

But, what about the "departing from your relative" part? We are not given an answer for that situation, but we are told that Abram wasn't allowed to proceed to the Promise Land until Tarah, his father, had passed away (Gen. 11:32, Acts 7:4). Essentially, Genesis 12: 1-3 becomes a reiteration of God's previous call to Abraham and the promises accompanying.

I must say, especially after chronicling the previous chapters of this book, Abraham's life's examples in the exercising of faith are refreshing. Sheepishly I say, I have no problem identifying with the ambiguity seen in his faith choices. I wonder how many times I've been called to walk by faith in a challenging way and only partially responding to the depth of the primary call. And, like Abraham, able to always find rationales and justifications for the partial obedience. We'll have more on this later.

At God's timing, Abram took Sarai and Lot, along with all their possessions and servants accumulated in Haran and proceeded on to the land of Canaan. "*And the Lord God appeared to Abram and said,* 'To *your descendants I will give this land.*' So, *he built an altar there to the Lord who had*

appeared to him". (Gen.12:5-7) There in Bethel they called upon the name of the Lord. We have no reference to the amount of time transpired where they enjoyed the fruits of their labor before the next challenge hit. And did it hit!

"*Now there was a famine in the land*". (Gen.12:10) Decision time for Abram, who was beyond 75 years and Sarai 65 years of age. Verdict in; we are going down to *Egypt*! Can't help but wonder. Was this the best solution? Did God bring the family from Ur to Bethel ('the house of God') to abandon them by not taking care of every need? God, surely, knew what they would face beforehand. Surely, He would "meet every need" they would experience.

Hear me well! I am certainly not criticizing Abram – I'm questioning. Chances are good, I would have made the same decision. Like most of us, I'd like to think I would have stayed and exercised great faith. But then reality takes hold and honesty sets in. For me this situation prompts a quandary: "How do I process decisions needed to be made when confronted by the need to appropriate faith"?

Do I merely examine the circumstances and determine the action taken solely by the surface discoveries; or deepen the investigation by searching Biblical specimens of how God has worked in the past. Using Abrams' plight as an example; and we find ourselves in a similar predicament; how would we proceed? Might we ask these questions?

1. Can God meet every need I might have? Yes! Phil. 4:19 Mt. 6:8
2. Has God fed others during a famine? Yes! 1 Kings 17: 1-24

3. Has God produced water in a drought? Yes! Ex. 17: 6-7 Nu. 20: 1-13

Now comes the most pertinent question – Am I ready to appropriate God's Word and lay my conviction on the line and boldly walk by faith and not by circumstances.

Our Lord has allowed Lana and I to live out such experiences of using God's Word as the basis for discovering His perfect will for our lives. I've mentioned how God called us into full time ministry – allow me to share the rest of the story.

For us, concluding, as to whether, it was God's perfect will to uproot the security we enjoyed as a family and venture out into the unknown was a daunting task. How can we know with utmost assurance that this was the call of God for our family. On the surface, it was easy to find numerous reasons not to proceed with the notion; perhaps it's just our egos going berserk. On the other hand, what if it is God's will for us.

Reminders of the formula we use for answers that seem elusive finally hit home. The process is relatively simple. Search the Scriptures for an example and bathe the principle in prayer – then wait. While perhaps not for everyone, God took us to one of my Biblical heroes, Gideon.

An angel of the Lord visited Gideon, challenging him to deliver Israel from the hand of the Midianites. Basically,

Gideon said (as I paraphrase). “Are you crazy? Look at me? Who am I to entrust such a task to? He then countered, “*If I have found favor in Thy sight, then show me a sign that is Thou who speaks to me*”. (Jud. 6:12-40) God, in His faithfulness, brought Gideon through a series of miraculous “signs” designed to build confidence in his spirit convincing him to heed the call. All of these got his attention and brought to his final request. Final proof would be in the proverbial “fleece before the Lord.”

We agreed with Gideon – put out a fleece before the Lord!

We prayed about how we would proceed; God was faithful to encourage us in the following way. Lana and I were to meet with the Pastor and his wife for lunch in Oakdale California. Since finances were of concern due to the lesser amount we would have to work with, we were inspired to contact the Pastor and have him write down on a piece of paper the most the church would be able to commit to. As well, we wrote on a piece of paper the least we would need.

I’ll never forget that meeting as both of us laid our little pieces of paper out on the table – they were to the dollar the same amount. Thank you, Lord! You’ve given the assurance needed! We said “Yes” to the call and haven’t looked back for these 45+ years.

Abram came to his conclusion on the matter and "*went down to Egypt to sojourn there*". (Gen.12:10-26) As we meditate on this passage, we could be inclined to think that he made the right choice in going. After all, didn't he come back as a rich man? Yes, I suppose! But, what about the lies he had to live out? What about the turmoil he caused to those in the land. What about the "*Egyptian maid whose name was Hagar*" (Gen.16: 1-16) that was brought back hidden among the spoils (a spoil Satan would use later, bringing into existence Ishmael).

At this juncture it's apparent Abram endured the consequences of the decisions made previously. He showed great strength and courage that bolstered his faith when he returned to the "*place of the altar*" (Gen.13:4). Added, the deliverance of Lot from the Kings of Sodom (Gen.14:1-17). Also, append his glorious encounter with king/priest Melchizedek. I would contend these are growth steps in faith. For when we reach chapter 17, and Abram is ninety-nine, God states, "No *longer shall your name be Abram, but your name shall be Abraham; I will make you the father of a multitude of nations.*" (Gen.17:1-4)

All these happenings brought Abraham to the apex of his life of faith, the willingness to sacrifice his son, Isaac. The New Testament writer James added his account of the faith of Abraham (Jms.2:18,23). '*Someone may well say, 'You have faith, and I have works; show me your works; and I will show you my faith by my works.'* Again: "*And Abraham believed God, and it was reckoned to him as righteousness," and he was called a friend of God.*

My Personal "Walk of Faith" Journal: Ch.5

1. Abraham journeyed into the "unknown" in response to God's calling. To a place unfamiliar and uncomfortable, a place of insecurity – yet, to a place of promise. Recalling the account (pg.27,28), how hard do you think it was for him to suddenly up-root he, and his family's, life forging into the 'unknown'?

____

____

____

____

Based on your level of faith right now, do you think you could have?

____

____

Would you be willing if God called you to the 'unknown'?

____

____

2. We concluded that Abraham partially obeyed in having his father accompany them on this adventure; Have you ever been in a place where 'full' obedience was required, and you only 'partially' obeyed the call?

____

____

____

____

What were the results?

____

____

What about the time you fully obeyed the call?

____

____

3. At the height of an unexpected crisis, we often have a tendency to rely on our own understanding (Proverbs 3: 5-7). We focus our eyes on the circumstances surrounding us; and make a conclusion based on the circumstances; and come to a decision according to our own thinking.

____

____

____

____

Would you say that you were ‘fully trusting God’?

____

____

What could be some steps you can take when the next crisis comes your way to avoid ‘walking by sight’ and instead “walk by faith”?

____

____

4. Write down three Bible verses that will encourage you to allow God to lead you instead of 'your own understanding'?

1.

2.

3.

CHAPTER SIX

Heb. 11: 17-19

" Parents Bolster Faith in Children "

"By faith Abraham, when he was tested, offered up Isaac; and he who had received the promises was offering up his only begotten son; it was he to whom it was said; 'IN ISAAC YOUR DESCENDANTS SHALL BE CALLED.' He considered that God is able to raise men even from the dead; from which he also received him back as a type."

Who likes to be tested? Or be challenged to make
a snap decision?

An event in Darlington, Maryland happened several years ago. Edith, a mother of eight, was coming home from a neighbor's house one Saturday afternoon. Things seemed too quiet as she walked across the from yard. Curious, she peered through the screen door and saw five of her children huddled together, concentrating on something. As she crept closer to them, trying to discover the center of their attention, she could not believe her eyes. Smack dab in the middle of the circle were five baby skunks. Edith screamed at the top of her voice, "Quick children...run!" Each kid grabbed a skunk and ran. (Swindoll; The Quest for Character, Multnomah).

Living by faith will often bring a disciple of Christ to a crossroad. Decisions must be made that can create lasting consequences, some painless to work through and some arduous. Father Abraham found himself in this situation, which represents the last dialogue from God to him. "*When he was tested*" (Heb.11:17; Gen.22:1) God said, "*take your son, your only son, whom you love, and go to the land* of Moriah; *and offer him there as a burnt offering on one of the mountains of which I will tell you.*" (Gen. 22:2)

(I wonder if his immediate muse was this?)

"But this is my only son!".

"I have waited for such a long time for this precious boy!"

"It was You who promised him and gave him to me!"

"Every hope and dream of mine is conditioned on him!"
"What is Sarah going to say?"

I have no way of knowing if any uncertainties ran through Abraham's mind as he contemplated God's appeal. I only know of those I might have called into question and pondered upon their consequences. Regardless of any possibilities that one might suggest, Abraham didn't seem to allow a single secular rumination to have its way. For the passage goes on to state," *So Abraham rose early in the morning and saddled his donkey....*" (Gen. 22:3)

God's word adds that Abraham arrived at the destination on the third day. So, here he is with Isaac, a couple of men who accompanied them, and the split wood, making their way to the location designated by God. "*And Abraham said to his young men, 'Stay here with the donkey, and I and the lad will go yonder; and we will worship and return to you*'". (Gen.22:5) Father Abraham wasn't positively sure just what the future held, but he was absolutely sure of Who held the future.

Would God, actually, allow this dad to suffer the agony of thrusting a knife into the flesh of his "only son?" If so, Dad knew his son would breathe again. As intriguing as any ponderings are concerning the gravity of the situation, I'm equally enthralled in the mind set of Isaac. What was he experiencing through this ordeal? We are, somewhat, privy to Abraham's walk of faith, but what about Isaac's? Dad had lived a long life, seasoned in the ways of the Lord. To what extent had Isaac grown in faith as he surveyed his father's journey of certainty in his God?

As a result of my study, I'm of the persuasion that Isaac was at least a teenager. Mature enough to fully assess the apparent dilemma, and strong enough to push back if there is an apparent danger to his person. With this in mind – walk with me as I presuppose how the thinking and conversation might have unfolded.

Abraham:	Isaac:
1. He told the young men – "*we will go yonder; we will worship and will return,*"	1. I don't understand all of what's going on here, but dad said, "*We will return.*"
2. He "*laid the wood on Isaac,*" then took the "*fire and the knife.*" "*They walked together.*'"	2. "*Behold, the fire and wood, where is the lamb*?" Time to worry? No! Dad said, "*God will provide a for Himself the lamb.*"
3. They arrived at the place God had directed them. Abraham "*built an altar, arranged the wood, bound his son, and laid him on the wood*".	3. Amazing; the absence of fear. Could Isaac rebel? Probably! No recorded responses here – his confidence was in his dad.
4. Dad "*stretched out his hand, and took the knife to slay his son, knowing,* "IN ISAAC YOUR DESCENDANTS SHALL BE CALLED." (Heb.11:18)	4. The bindings – the wood – witnessing the knife about to be thrust in his chest. No panic on dad's face – thus Isaac's heart is calm before the Lord.

"An angel caught Abraham's attention; he saw the ***"ram caught in the thicket".*** It became the sacrifice. ***The Lord will provide"*** -Jehovah Jireh. Gen. 22: 13,14

On occasion, I have asked myself: Is faith more "taught" or "caught"? Both! Faith, as the Apostle Paul exhorts, does "*come by hearing and the hearing by the word of Christ*". (Rom.10:17) But then, it's also 'caught' from those who have been called to experience challenges that have allowed them to walk by faith. We do possess a tendency toward searching for an example to follow from the life's choices of others and from our own previous experiences.

We find ourselves extremely blessed to live in a time where models of faith are at our fingertips. The Scriptures are filled with peoples' testimonials exhibiting their trust in God's solemn procedures. We've already addressed some in this publication. Then, extra blessings are prevalent with family and friends exhibit their walk-in faith for us to duplicate.

I regret I must add this truth - the opposite is also prevalent. Where there is an absence in the execution of living by faith, thus living by sight, antithetical outcomes can arise.

In the previous chapter we addressed the fact that Abraham chose to go into Egypt during the famine that overcame the land of Canaan. I suggested that this was God's permissive will and not His perfect will. I'm of the persuasion that Abraham ("Dad") shared the account with his son many times, accenting the godly choices and those questionable ones.

So, here we are in Genesis 26 verse one – another famine – more choices to be made – this time for Isaac. Did the accounts of his father penetrate his mind? Of course, we have no way of knowing, we just know his dad had a great influence on him. Whatever his thinking at the time, "*the Lord appeared to him and said, 'Do not go down to Egypt, stay in the land of which I will tell you'*. (26: 2) – "*So Isaac lived in Gerar*" (26:6). This was certainly a godly choice. Good job Isaac.

But we continue in Genesis 26, verse seven. "*When the men of the place asked about his wife, he said, 'She is my sister', for he was afraid to say, ' my wife, thinking, the men of the place might kill me on account of Rebekah, for she is beautiful.*" Sound familiar? Yes! It's almost identical to what Abraham had thought and said in Egypt. Not so good Isaac.

"*And it came about, when he had been there a long time, Abimelech looked out through a window, and saw, and behold Isaac was caressing his wife, Rebekah.*" (vs.8) Good job Isaac.

Why did you say she was your sister when surely, she is your wife, asked Abimelech? "*Because I might die on account of her.*" *Abimelech said, "What is this you have done to us? One of the people might have easily lied with your wife, and you would have brought guilt upon us.*" Again, so reminiscent of the events involving 'Dad'. Not so good Isaac.

Suppose this can serve as a reminder of the important influence we as fathers, and grandfathers can have upon our families. Teaching Biblical truth is vital in our goal to strengthen the resolve of every member of each coming under our influence. But, also, are the principles that will be 'caught' along the way due to our righteous living. When we examine Isaac's parenting skills with Jacob and Esau (Gen.25-27), can we say that he learned the principles of fatherhood? Exercising faith that captivates?

My Personal "Walk of Faith" Journal: Ch. 6

1. Read through Genesis 22: 1 – 18. Identify, and list, the ways in this account correlates with the story of Christ's crucifixion. (Example: "Take now your son, your only son." John 3:16)

____

____

____

____

2. As you think back over your time as a believer, would you consider your "faith" being more "taught" or more "caught," or equally both? (Explain your response.)

____

____

____

____

3. *"For whom He foreknew, He also predestined to become conformed to the image of His Son."* (Rom. 8:29) It is God's desire for each of us to become more and more like Jesus, because He is our perfect example – the Father's will for us. This is an important process we must not neglect. This process requires time spent in God's Word; thus are "taught" the ways of Christ and (remember) it's God's way of growing us in faith (Rom. 10: 17).

____

____

____

____

As you evaluate your current "faith" journey, what might be the areas you need to become more Christ-like?

____

____

4. What family member or friend has been a positive example for you because of their "walk by faith?"

How has this affected your faith walk?

____

____

In what way/ways would you like to duplicate their faith walk?

____

____

5. To those that personally apply to you; respond to these questions.

What kind of example am I to my family? (Husband/wife, Kids, Siblings, Grandkids, etc.)

____

____

What about the friends you attend church with?

____

____

What about your friends outside the faith?

____

____

6. Abraham is certainly a very good example of "walking by faith" – in his walk he "grew in faith." It is a lifelong process! It's a growth into spiritual maturity that leads to willingly giving up anything we once held on to as treasures. Imagine, a willingness to sacrifice in such a way as Abraham laying his "only son" before the Lord.

____

____

Are you "growing" in faith as you grow older? Or standing still? Or weakening?

____

____

CHAPTER SEVEN

Heb. 11: 21, 22

" Faith Discerns God's Activity "

"By faith Jacob, as he was dying, blessed each of the sons of Joseph, and worshiped, leaning on the top of his staff. By faith Joseph, when he was dying, made mention of the sons of Israel, and gave orders concerning his bones."

Heb. 11: 21, 22

One of the traits escorting a person endeavoring to live by 'faith' is 'endurance'. In Webster's 1828 dictionary it was defined as "A bearing or suffering: a continuing under pain or distress without resistance, or without sinking or yielding to pressure, sufferance, or patience".

For me an example of this truth is Joseph. Imagine being asked to prevail through all the 'suffering and distress' confronting his integrity and moral strength. In the end he merely states to his brethren "*It was not you who sent me here, but God*" (Gen.45:8);

> "***You meant evil against me, but God meant it for good***"
>
> (Gen.50: 20).

As we peruse the character of Joseph's life, we can acquire knowledge and instruction Concerning our own spiritual maturity.

One senses an air of pride in Joseph as he flaunts his "*varicolored tunic*" (Gen.37:3) around his brothers. Their take was "*they saw their father loved him (Joseph) more than all his brothers, so they hated him,* (they were) *not on friendly terms*" (Gen.37:4). Why wouldn't a conspicuous 'air of pride' prevail in Joseph. His dad, Jacob, made it known to all that Joseph's mom, Rachel, was loved more than the moms of the other boys. (Preferential treatment begets preferential treatment).

I wonder; did the brothers have an attitude that said, "We don't get mad, we get even." Whatever, the more confrontive Joseph became, the angrier the brothers became. Joseph gave an account of his dreams that implied his brothers would "bow" down to him. His brothers said, "*Are you actually going to reign (rule) over us? So, they hated him even more.*" (Gen.37:5-11)

If that wasn't enough, Joseph divulged another dream that included Jacob prompting this question from dad; "*What is this dream you have had? Shall I and your mother and your bothers actually come and bow ourselves down before you to the ground?*" (Gen.37:10)

Way to go Joseph, you've managed to alienate your entire family! But these words didn't originate from the heart of Joseph, but from the Lord. Most likely, he didn't fully comprehend the impact his words would have on his family. Apparently, he felt compelled to speak the trues he had received from the Most High God - regardless of the consequences.

> This presents a lesson for us! It takes great faith to speak God's life-giving principles to a darkened world. Jesus warned this, we will be "*persecuted for the sake of righteousness....(people) will cast insults at us....and say all kinds of evil against us falsely, on account of Him" But rejoice and be glad, for your reward in heaven is great*". (Matt.5:10,11,12)

Presumably, Joseph didn't anticipate the 'consequences.' He was approaching his brothers from a distance; they saw him and "*plotted against him to put him to death. They said to one another, 'here comes the dreamer! ...let us kill him and throw into one of the pits; and we will say, 'A wild beast devoured him.'* (Gen.37:18-36) This idea was debated by the brothers and ultimately it was decided they would keep him in a pit, and he could be sold to the Ishmaelites. Convincing Jacob would be easy – kill an animal, saturate the tunic with blood and devise a lie that Jacob would readily accept? He did and mourned for him greatly.

So, here's the teen-ager Joseph, in the possession of the Midianites headed for Egypt. Can we wonder – did he yell and throw a tantrum? Scream out, "Why me"? Vow to get even? I wonder, did he already know,

"You meant evil against me, but God meant it for good."

Now in Egypt, in the house of an Egyptian officer, Potiphar, Joseph became very successful. Potiphar saw greatness in Joseph and "*made him overseer over his house...everything he owned was put in his charge*". The only exception? His wife! (As it should be). Apparently, the wife wasn't listening, and she pursued Joseph saying, "*Lie with me.*" (Gen.39:1-23) This went on day after day; and day after day he said no. She got ticked off – lied to her husband Potiphar by accusing Joseph of infidelity – her hubby believed it, after all, there was his robe, and had Joseph thrown in jail.

How could God allow this to happen to me? "I chose to remain pure in Your sight O Lord. I make decisions matching who I am in You. I'm now suffering the consequences wrongly." Do we think these, and other comments were made by Joseph? Or did he discern?

"You meant evil against me, But God meant it for good."

Here Joseph is in prison, "*But the Lord was with Joseph and extended kindness to him and gave him favor in the sight of the chief jailer.*" (*Gen.39:21*) *Joseph was to supervise* everything in the jail, even the prisoners. And the "*Lord made him prosper*". Faith discerns God's hand in everything He allows into one's life.

A great man of faith, George Muller, once stated, "God delights to increase the faith of His children. We ought, instead of wanting no trials before victory, no exercise for patience, to be willing to take them from God's hand as a means. I say – and say it deliberately – trials, obstacles, difficulties, and sometime defeats, are very good food of faith."

"Well done, good and faithful servant, you were faithful in a few things, I will put you in charge in many things".

(Matt. 25: 23)

Joseph was found faithful in every situation he found himself, thus God increased his opportunities to exercise more faithfulness. God is moving him from jail to Pharaoh's house. It's so interesting how God positioned Joseph to enable so great an adjustment to take place. (Make no mistake; God employs similar circumstances in our lives to further our faithfulness.)

"Pharaoh was furious with his two officials, the chief cupbearer and the chief baker. He put them in confinement in the house of the captain of the bodyguard, in the jail, the same place where Joseph was imprisoned. The captain of the bodyguard put Joseph in charge of them, and he took care of them, and they were confined for some time." (Gen.40:1-4) One particular day Joseph approached the two officials under his care. Viewing the sadness on their faces, he solicited the problem. Both had a dream on the same night, and there was no one to interpret. *"Joseph said to them, 'Do not interpretations belong to God? Tell them to me, please.'"* (Gen.40:7,8)

The two related their dreams and were eager to receive the meanings. Joseph listened to their testimonies; God gave him the interpretations. "<u>I have good news and bad news</u>". To the cupbearer he said, *"within three days Pharaoh will lift up your head and restore you to your office."* (Gen.40:8-15) He added this nuance, '*remember me when you are serving Pharaoh*'.

Then he focused on the baker. Sorry to inform you, but you are history. "*Within three days Pharaoh will lift up your head from you and will hang you on a tree; and the birds will eat your flesh off.*" (Gen.40:16-22) It takes great faith to remain honest in touchy situations.

> There was, also, some 'bad news' for Joseph. ***"The chief cupbearer did not remember Joseph but forgot him."***
>
> (Gen.40:23)

Another opportunity to question circumstances.
Anger? Frustration? Discouragement?

I believe he exclaimed: **"You meant evil against me – but God meant it for good."**

Probably not fully understanding God's plan, Joseph seemed to prevail through the incidents without annoyance even though he remained in jail for the next two years. But God, knew what He was doing and gave a dream to Pharaoh at just the proper time. Pharaoh was "*troubled*, about the dream, *and sent and called for all the magicians of Egypt, and all the wise men. All were wise* men. *And Pharaoh told them his dreams, but there was no one who could interpret them to Pharaoh*".(Gen.41:1-12) Then, as God would have it, the cupbearer shared his dream experience with Pharaoh and pointed to the ministry of Joseph – he finally remembered.

"*Pharaoh sent and called for Joseph ... and said, 'I have had a dream, but no one can interpret it; and I have heard it said about you, that when you hear a dream, you can interpret it'. Joseph answered saying, 'It is not in me; God will give Pharaoh a favorable answer.*" (Gen.41:14-16)

In Genesis 41: 16-41 we read of Pharaoh's dream as he divulged it to Joseph. Then Joseph, in response, communicated the meaning of the dream and details on how these night visions were to be discharged. The dynamic of the message must have been intriguing to Joseph. Even though he had no idea what the future held, he must have speculated about it. Also, I wonder if he had begun to imagine what his actions would be.

The essence of Joseph's report was: There shall be "*seven years of great abundance*" and after them "*seven years of famine will come*". Joseph, not only, imparted the particulars concerning the time of abundance, but counseled Pharaoh on how best to precede. Joseph's consultation included: "*appoint overseers in charge of the land*" *and* "*gather all the food and grain in the good years*" and "*let the food become a reserve* for the seven years of famine". Pharaoh said to Joseph; "*Since God has informed you of all this, there is no one so discerning and wise as you are*".

Here, Joseph, at thirty years of age, is "*clothed in a garment of fine linen... given Pharaoh's signet ring*" representing authority, second in charge of all Egypt.

God knew, absolutely, that His plan included depositing His people, Israel, in Egypt. Since this was His blueprint, He worked out the details using the willing instrument He could trust to accomplish the stratagem. Joseph is the effectual servant of the Lord when "*all the people of the earth came to Egypt to buy grain from Joseph.....when Jacob saw that there was grain in Egypt, he said to his sons, 'why are you staring at one another?'....I have heard there is grain in Egypt; go down there and buy some for us in that place"......"The ten brothers of Joseph went down to buy grain.*" Joseph's brothers were among the many who came to Joseph to fulfill their needs, for he was the "*ruler over the land....And Joseph's brothers came and bowed down to him with their faces to the ground.*" (Gen.42:1-38)

Joseph revealed himself to his brothers, which became an emotional time for all. Their eyes were opened and fully discerning of how God had carried out His will in each of their lives. Hindsight is a breeze compared to approaching each new day that can run into years without apprehending fully the perfect will of God. Calamity can be part of how our Lord works His will in our lives.

How do we react in uncomfortable situations?

How about when we are asked to wait a while?

When we are sure we are being taken advantage of?

When do we see apostasy grip the hearts of loved ones?

When it seems like God has abandoned us?

These, and others, require living by faith. "*Yet those who wait for the Lord will gain new strength; they will mount up with wings like eagles, they will run and not get tired, they will walk and not become weary*. (Isa. 40:31)

In every situation they will be able to honestly declare:

"You meant evil against me – But God meant it for good."

My Personal "Walk by Faith" journal: Ch. 7

1. Preferential treatment can occur in many places; the home, at school, the workplace, friendships, etc.

How do you react when others are getting preferential treatment over you?

____

____

____

How do you act when you are favored over others?

____

____

2. Have you ever had someone intentionally hurt you in some way?

____

____

How did you handle the situation?

Looking back on the dilemma, can you assess that, while it was meant as evil against you, God allowed it for your good?

3. God has not promised that we would be void of difficult times; however, He has promised He would always go through those times with us – never forsaken by Him – as He was with Joseph.

Write about a difficult time in which God made His presence known to you in the midst of the dilemma.

4. How does knowing that God delights in increasing the faith of His children encourage you in your journey of Faith?

___

___

___

5. God had a special for Joseph; and God has a special plan for you to carry out His perfect will. What do you think God's perfect plan for you is in your "walk of faith" right now?

___

___

___

6. What is going on in your life at this time that is requiring you to walk by faith?

___

___

___

7. Joseph's faith, during his trials, becomes a great example for us today. What have you gleaned from Joseph's life's ordeals that you plan to apply to the hardships you might be asked to face.

CHAPTER EIGHT

Heb. 11: 23 –29

" Faith Makes the Difficult Choices Seem Easy "

"By faith Moses, *when he was born, was hidden for three months by his parents, because they saw he was a beautiful child; and they were not afraid of the king's edict. By faith* Moses, *when he had grown up, refused to be called the son of* Pharaoh's *daughter; choosing rather to endure ill-treatment with the people of* God, *than to enjoy the pleasures of sin;*

considering the reproach of Christ greater than the treasures of Egypt; for he was looking to the reward. By faith he left Egypt, not fearing the wrath of the king; for he endured, as seeing Him who is unseen. By faith he kept the Passover and the sprinkling of the blood, so that he who destroyed the firstborn might not touch them. By faith they passed through the Red Sea as though they were passing through dry land; and the Egyptians, when they attempted it, were drowned."

(Heb. 11: 23-29)

It is obvious that God had His hand upon the life of Moses from the very beginning. Even though Pharaoh had ordered God's people, saying, "*Every son who is born to you* are *to cast into the Nile, and every daughter you are to keep alive.*" (Ex.1:22) Regardless of what men may, in their own notorious way exhorting ungodly ignorance, proclaim, when God's hand is upon His servant, the outcome is miraculous. Such is the first forty years of Moses' life. An initial walk into faith.

Snuggling in a 'wicker basket' that had been deposited in the Nile River – the very place other newborn boys had perished – he is discovered by Pharaoh's daughter. The basket is opened, and a crying baby boy, obviously a Hebrew, is now in the hands of what, seemingly, represented the 'enemy'. Perhaps, she surprised herself, but instead of casting the baby aside or taking him to daddy, she embraced the child and discovered how this precious little boy could be cared for. By whom? The mother, of course, who would even receive 'wages' for her effort. "*And the child grew, and she brought him to Pharaoh's daughter, and he became her son. And she named him Moses, and said, 'Because I drew him out of the water.'*" (Ex.2:10)

For the next, almost forty years Moses was "*educated in all the learning of Egyptians, and he was a man of power in words* and *deeds.*" (Acts 7:20-24) It was at this juncture in his life, "*approaching the age of forty, it* <u>entered his mind</u> *to visit his brethren, the sons of Israel.... He saw one of them being treated unjustly.... he defended him....and took vengeance....by striking down the Egyptian.*" Obviously, this didn't sit too well with Pharaoh and his instinct was to kill Moses, but Moses fled from his presence to Midian.

> The statement above. it "entered his mind" encourages us to examine an important Biblical principle. It was God who brought His will to the <u>mind</u> of Moses – it was Moses who had a mind to receive God's will. "*For the mind set on the flesh is death, but the mind set on the Spirit is life and peace. Because the mind set on the flesh is hostile toward God.*" (Rom.8:7) We are called to be "*of the same mind*" as Christ. Paul accented his exhortation by adding, "*let this attitude (mind) be in you which is also in Christ Jesus.*" (Phil.2:1-5) It's summed up like this, "*Set your mind on the things above, not on the things on earth.*" (Col.3:2) God, not only wants control of our mind, but needs control to have access at any time – so He can lead us into walking in His perfect will living by faith.

We now enter Midian that represents the next forty years where God is preparing Moses to lead His people out of Egypt and into the Promised Land. We can rightfully assume that he was being led by God to choose the Midianites where to find asylum. They were children of Abraham – relatives of Israel. When Sarah had died, *Abraham "took another wife whose name was Keturah, who bore Midian."* (Gen.25:1-4) Now, the ungodly principles Moses received from the Egyptians had to be extinguished, preparing his heart and mind to be directed to the Living God and administering his living by faith.

It didn't take long for Moses to become noticed in the new land; soon, he encountered the seven daughters of the priest of Midian. Apparently, while the girls were attempting to fill their containers with water for their father's flock, enemies approached venturing to thwart the tasks of the daughters. Then "*Moses stood up and helped them*" (Ex.2:11-25) – he came to the rescue - he saved the day. The elated maidens related the story to their father. Jethro, and he replied, "*Where is he...? Why have you left the man behind? Invite him to have something to eat.*"

A new relationship is initiated that depicts Moses' willingness to "*dwell with the man, and he (the man) gave his daughter Zipporah to Moses.*" The Scripture goes on the state that a son was born who was named Gershom. Next scene: Moses is pasturing his father-in-law, Jethro, flock on Mount Horeb. He is now about eighty years of age. As curious as we might be as to all the events that must have happened, we can only imagine about the details, but we can know God was in full control in His work of preparing Moses to walk by faith and not by sight.

On Mount Horeb;

"*The angel of the Lord appeared to him in a blazing fire from the midst of a bush, Moses looked, and behold, the bush was burning with fire, yet was not consumed. Moses said, 'I must. turn aside, and see this marvelous sight, why the bush has not burned us.'. The Lord saw that he turned aside to look and called to him from the midst of the bush, and said, 'Moses, Moses!' Moses said, 'Here I am.' God said, 'Do not come near here, remove your sandals from your feet. For the place on which you are standing is holy ground.' God also said, 'I am the God of your father, the God of Abraham, the God of Isaac, and the God of Jacob,' Then Moses hid his face, for he was afraid to look at God,*" (Ex.3:1-6) God had gotten the attention of Moses and was ready to further their relationship.

In future conversation with Moses, God said, "I have a plan. I'm sending you to Pharaoh." Now comes a series of testing prior to him standing at the water's edge of the Red Sea, with his staff in hand, about to exercise great faith waving it over the waters, expecting God to miraculously divide the billows before all the children of Israel. Chapters 3 - 11 of Exodus (which I encourage you to read) we are encountered with these probes of how he advances in faith.

Before being given the opportunity to exercise 'great faith', God will generally bring us through times of less intense testing to aide our personal growth in our faith walks. Illustration.

In 1986 God called us from serving in the camping ministry back into a Pastoral position in California's north coast. After we had been a candidate there, the nice people contacted us offering the assignment. The church had waned in size to the point where the future looked very bleak. There comment was, "We really want you to come but we can't remunerate in any way". Now, don't get me wrong, we do not require much, but we had gotten use to eating, paying bills, and being clad. So, what are we going to do?

The mind games started! Where we are is quite secure and moving is a hassle. Where will we live? Don't know! How will we make ends meet? Don't know! What about the adjustments? No idea! Many practical questions ensued - but what do we think God desires? After much deliberating and seeking the face of God, we decided I could be a bi-vocational servant of the Lord – so, "yes, we will accept the call.

Less than a week went by, two people approach us saying, "We'll up pick your salary for a year." What an answer to our prayers and evidence that God honors our living by faith. Miracles continued; seven months later we were able to tell these blessed doners they could earmark their giving to other needs, for the Lord had blessed the ministry to where our needs were being met and able to add a fulltime youth pastor to our staff. All our quandaries were answered. I can't even imagine where we would be had we said "no" to God. * God had worked patiently and persuasively over a period of time, in a myriad of ways, to aide in our faith walk.

"*I will send you to Pharaoh*", God states. (Is Moses thinking; "at least it's a different Pharaoh, not the one who wanted to kill me.") Moses, being human, began his own interrogation.

Moses said, "*Who am I that I should go to Pharaoh?*" **God countered, "Certainly I will be with you."** (Ex. 3:1-22)

Moses responded, "*I'm going to the sons of Israel, what if they ask,* "*What is His name?*" **Say, "I AM WHO I AM" - Say to them, "I AM has sent me to you".** At this point, God went on to exhort; take the elders of Israel and go to the king of Egypt seeking permission to leave Egypt. He will rebel against your plea; but I will miraculously evoke him to evict you. Plus, they will willingly relinquish many valuable items; to where they will feel they have been plundered.

Moses answered, "*What if they don't believe me, or listen to what I say?*" The Lord replied, "**The staff in your hand? – Throw it down to the ground!"** It became a serpent. The Lord continued, **"Stretch out your hand and grasp it by the tail."** It became his staff – God used this to help convince Pharaoh to "drive the people out of the Land."

Moses: "*Please, Lord, I have never been eloquent....I am slow of speech and slow of tongue.*" **"I, even, I will be in your mouth, and teach you what to say."** God finally had to allow the brother of Moses to speak due to the lack of faith in the heart of Moses. (Ex. 4:1-31)

Sound familiar? Is this the essence of faith? "*The assurance of things hoped for, the conviction (evidence) of things not seen? God says,* "MOVE" – *we say* – "BUT........"

Through the ten plagues wrought upon pharaoh and people of Egypt, God schools Moses in becoming stalwart in conviction that he can trust the Word of God. First! Imagine witnessing water being turned to blood by striking the Nile with the 'staff'. Second! Take the staff and wave it over the river, ponds, and creeks and deal with thousands of frogs.

Third! With the staff strike the dust and blanket man and beast with gnats. We must take notice that the magicians could not counter what only God can do – Create. The frogs were already created, the magicians only brought them forth – likewise the water in the Nile.

Fourth! This, also, becomes a pivotal growth factor for Moses. Up to this plague Aaron had taken the lead, now Moses will be the voice for God throughout the remaining decrees. We are given evidence of his maturing character.

Fifth! Again, Pharaoh refused to let God's people go so God smite Egypt's livestock with severe pestilence. All of the livestock of Egypt died – the livestock of Israel did not.

Sixth! Here we have another important prototype of God's grace as He advances Moses' faith. He will allow His servant to take a more active role in this plague. Moses will take handfuls of soot, throw it to the sky, and as it covers the people it becomes boils, even on the magicians.

Seventh! Hail. Eighth! Locusts. Ninth! Darkness. All similar in application.

Tenth! We must look at this plague in a special way. Our Sovereign Creator, God is ruler overall and demonstrates His authority demanding our honor and respect. The plague? "*All the firstborn in the land of Egypt shall die, from the firstborn of the Pharaoh who sits on the throne, even to the firstborn of the slave girl who sits behind the millstone, all the firstborn of cattle as well."* (Ex.11:5) Next, we see God's grace – the Passover is instituted – instruction given.

The people were to take an '*unblemished male lamb a year old*' or '*from the goats*' and '*take some of the blood and put it on the doorposts and on the lintel of the houses*'. God added, '*I will go through* the *land of Egypt – I will strike down the firstborn of the land of Egypt – I will execute judgment. But 'when I see the blood, I will pass over you, no plague will befall you.*'

Imagine the electrifying emotions of the, some, two million people as they assemble their belongings, especially the silver, gold, and clothing 'plundered' from the Egyptians. Upon being in bondage four hundred years, and now unconstrained, every soul rejoicing in how God has demonstrated His power and authority. But where are we headed? Is there a map to our destination?

There is God's version of having a GPS system – "A *pillar of cloud by day to lead them on the way, and a pillar of fire by night to give them light, that they might travel by day and by night."* (Ex,13:17-22) Even with all the miraculous demonstrations of power in setting them free, and now being led by a cloud and fire, and Moses in the lead; they "*became very frightened.*"

The ominous scene? Pharaoh's army behind them – the Red Sea before them! They evaluate the situation: unfortunately, like a human would be void of faith rendering spiritual eyes. The discourse from their lack of faith, "*Why have you dealt with us this way, bringing us out of Egypt?*" Didn't we say, "*Leave us alone that we might serve the Egyptians? For it would have been better to serve them than to die in the wilderness.*"

Moses also assesses the dilemma, but with spiritual eyes of faith in a mighty God, and retorts; "*Do not fear! Stand by and see the salvation of the Lord which He will accomplish for you today; for the Egyptians whom you have seen today. You will never see them again forever. The Lord will fight for you while you keep silent.*" (Ex.14:10-14)

<u>Why is it? People can survey an identical scene and arrive at contrasting resolutions!</u> One resolves to question with fear – one resolves to have confident solutions. It's my persuasion that Moses had availed himself to be discipled in the Lord. His Master had lovingly and patiently nurtured his faith walk. * Our Lord is willing, as well, to nurture us to live by faith and not by sight.*

So, here we are at the bank of the Red Sea, and in my estimation, we witness an incredible miracle, perhaps the greatest in the Old Testament. Moses is confident because he has listened and responded to God's tutelage when He stated, "*lift up your staff and stretch out your hand over the sea and divide it, and the sons of Israel shall go through in the midst of the sea on dry land.*" (Ex.14:15-21)

Not fully cognizant of the permeating musings on Moses' heart, as a human, though, I imagine what it must have been like to 1. Hear the groanings of the people; and 2. See the threats of the Egyptians; then 3. Survey the waters of the sea. But Moses "*stretched out his hand over the sea.*" (Ex.14:21) 'Sure, hope this works!' - 'What if it doesn't?' – 'How is this going to make me look?' – 'What if I do something wrong?' – 'What if I don't have enough faith?'

> Doubt can be a powerful emotion. (1828 Websters Dictionary) "To waver or fluctuate in opinion; to hesitate; to be in suspense; to be in uncertainty; to be undetermined."
>
> God exhorts; "*Have faith in God. Truly I say to you, whoever says to this mountain, (representing the, seemingly, impossible) Be taken up and cast into the sea, and does not doubt in his heart, but believes that what he says is going to happen, it shall have granted him.*" (Mk.11:22,23)
>
> Doubt: opposite of faith, trust, security, conviction, and reliability.

If any 'doubt' was present, Moses gained victory over it – with outstretched hand over the sea, "*the Lord swept the sea back by a strong east wind all night, and turned the sea into dry land, so the waters were divided. And the sons of Israel went through the midst of the sea on dry land, and the waters were like a wall to them on their right hand and on their left.*" (Ex.14:21,22) But God wasn't quite finished, for He, "*Returned the waters and covered the chariots and the horsemen, even Pharaoh's entire army that had gone into the sea after them; not even one remained.*" (Ex.14:28-31) Also, God allowed the people to see the Egyptians dead on the shore. And how God had saved Israel by His great power; and they 'feared' and 'believed' in the Lord and in Moses, His servant. *What if 'doubt' had had the victory? A repulsive thought! *

I don't remember where I heard this: Billie was in the third grade and his teacher was explaining this incredible event. She stated, however, it wasn't a miracle for they walked across on a stone shelf; the water was only two inches deep. Little Billie shouted out. 'Awesome miracle! What a display of power! Would have loved to have been there'. The teacher asked, 'What miracle?" Billie retorted,

'Pharaoh and all his army and all the horses drowned in two inches of water'. Awesome!

This solitary event would turn over in Moses' mind for the next forty years as the people were confined to a wilderness wandering. Water would flow from a rock – food would appear miraculously – discernment was at his disposal for all occasions. The people continued to gripe and complain, there were 'sea like' challenges continually, enemies were ever lurking ready to do battle. Through it all, Moses remained stalwart in his resolve. He was chosen to be given God's Law personally, to be God's sole spokesman to the people, yet remained subservient in all manner. It was his humility that prompted God's choosing him for service, for it is written, "*Moses was very humble, more than any man who was on the face of the earth.*" (Num.12:3)

Moses is such an ominous figure of Scripture, Peter, James and John must have been enrapt to witness the transfiguration of Christ. If Christ alone weren't enough to see, Moses added to the electrifying activity, along with Elijah (Lk.9:28-35). We consider also that Moses will be one of the Super Witnesses during the tribulation period, along with Elijah (Rev.11:4-6)

We who have come to faith in Jesus as our Savior and Lord will one day bask in His presence along with Moses and Elijah. My prayer for you is that you will be there also.

My Personal "Walk By Faith" Journal: Ch.8

---

1. What are some specific things that you can point to show how God has had His hand upon your life from the very beginning of your life?

____

____

____

____

2. What spiritual discipline or disciplines are you currently appropriating to keep "your mind set on things above?"

____

____

____

____

3. Has God ever used an extraordinary event in your life to get your attention to further your relationship with Him?

____

____

IF so, describe the incident.

____

____

How did the event change your life?

____

____

In what ways did it advance your faith?

____

____

4. Are you in a spiritual position where you are hearing when the Holy Spirit speaks?

____

____

Are you hearing a calling from Him to take a step into the unknown?

Are you like Moses and making excuses for not answering the call?

Or are you, in spite of your fears, trusting the Lord and moving forward?

5. In what ways is God lovingly and patiently nurturing you to "live by faith and not sight?"

6. Satan often attacks believers with doubts and fears.

How do you deal with doubt and fear in your life when they come?

____

____

Write out two Scriptures that you can "stand" on to curb doubts and fears.

____

____

____

____

CHAPTER NINE

Heb. 11: 30, 31

" Faith Fosters Unlimited Possibilities "

"By faith the walls of Jericho fell down, after they had been encircled for seven days. By faith Rahab the harlot did not perish along with those who were disobedient, after she had welcomed the spies in peace."

When our youngest daughter, Amy, was but an infant, the pastor of the Church where I was an associate would sit her in his hand and lift her up as high as he could. Without any apparent manifestation of fear; her face beaming with elation; she would giggle with delight, thoroughly enjoying the thrill as I would a roller coaster ride. As much amusement as she was feeling, her mom was looking on in horror.

Such is the principle of walking by faith. Amy's stage in life, and experience within it, had shielded her from any knowledge leading to anticipation. While her mom, at her stage in life, with her experiences, knew what potentially could happen, and expressed her anxiety. Personal occurrences can, very often, dictate a level of expectancy based on what 'might' take place. It is very possible for our imagination to overreact in fear, instead of reacting in faith.

Joshua might have responded similarly when he viewed the rapid waters of the Jordan, but he was discipled by the Lord through Moses. We find that as Moses was being tested in his walk, Joshua was being trained. He was on the mount – witnessed the plagues – walked the sea on dry land – drank water from the rock – fought spiritual battles – and was ready when God's call came for him to serve. Then the Words of God were added, "*Every place on which the sole of your foot treads, I have given to you, just as I have spoken to Moses....No man will be able to stand before you, just as I have been with Moses, I will*

be with you; I will not fail you or forsake you....Only be strong and very courageous; be careful to do according to all the law which Moses My servant commanded you; do not turn from it to the right or to the left, so that you may have success wherever you go." (Joshua 1:3-9)

As Moses stood before the Red Sea, Joshua stood at the bank of the Jordan River contemplating his first test. It seemed to imitate the Sea experience, but this was different.

Joshua was instructed to "*stand still in the Jordan....and it will come about when the soles of the priests who carry the ark of the Lord, the Lord of all the earth, shall rest in the waters of the Jordan, the waters of the Jordan will be cut off, and the waters which are flowing down from above shall stand in one heap*. Joshua conveyed God's message, and sure enough, the waters rose up in one heap. " *And the priests who carried the ark of the covenant stood firm on dry ground in the middle of the Jordan while all Israel crossed on dry ground, until all the nation had finished crossing the Jordan.*" (Josh.3: 7-17)

Here-in lies another principle of 'walking by faith'.

There are times (i.e., Moses) when God will urge us to 'wait' upon Him as He details out the steps for us to take. The miracle will happen without asking us to initiate anything, thus keeping us from (symbolically) getting our feet wet.

Other times (i.e., Joshua) He enhances our test by directing us to move toward the miracle. Exercising our step of faith, getting our feet wet, prompts Him to initiate the remaining steps to secure the miracle.

Both are God ordained. Both bring Him glory. Both are blessings for us.

Joshua must have been anxious to impound the Promised Land, but God explained that *"within three days you would cross the Jordan* " (Joshua.1:11) Apparently, at this time he chose to secretly send two spies *"to view the land, especially Jericho... The spies went and came into the house of Rahab and lodged there."* (Joshua.2:9)

Without sharing much in the way of details, the writer of Hebrews simply declares Rahab to be among the *"obedient"* in Jericho and *"she welcomed the spies in peace."* Not sure of the connection, but she hid the Israelites from the city's leadership. When word hit the ears of the king of Jericho; he ordered her to bring them to him. She told him, *"The men came to me, but I don't know where they were from."* She hid them on the roof of her home, all the time purging herself in the process. Why would she go out on a limb for these men? Without justifying her actions or deferring any guilt of diluting the truth (Josh.2:3-11), I really believe her heart was sincere before the Lord. Afterall, she prioritized the safety of the spies because she revered their Lord and God as Jehovah and Elohim. She couldn't allow any threat to come upon them from an enemy.

Again, the writer of Hebrews added, "*By faith Rahab...*" Her testimony to the men included, *"I know that the Lord has given you the land....all the inhabitants of the land have melted away before you"*. She went on to relate how that they were aware of the crossing of the Red Sea and other miracles that caused, *"our hearts to be melted and no courage remained...for the Lord your God, He is God in heaven above and on earth below."* Rahab asked that she and her family would be spared as she lowered the men through a window by a rope.

Her belief in the only true God would prompt her actions. Was she rewarded? She is included in the genealogy of Jesus (Matt.1:5). This illustrates how our faith can influence others!

Safe and sound in the 'Promise Land" It's time for the second test. Take Jericho! How? It's reported the outside wall was thirty feet high and six feet thick. Then about fifteen feet in distance from the outside wall was another wall also thirty feet in height – this wall was twelve feet in width (where the houses were like Rahab's). Because Joshua had sent in some men to spy out the land, he was aware of the challenges that faced them in 'tearing down that wall'. We are left to wonder if Joshua gaped at the structure and dwelt on the circumstances set before him; or was he able to remove the apparent odds before him and focus on the Lord's victory.

It was the Lord that said to Joshua, "*See, I have given Jericho into your hand, with its king and valiant warriors,*" with the following instructions. (I wonder if the Lord inferred these thoughts into the heart of Joshua: 'Put your trust into My plan – don't question My methods even though they seem ridiculous'). "*You shall march around the city, all the men of war circling the city once. You shall do so for six days...seven priests shall carry seven trumpets of rams' horns before the ark; then on the seventh day you shall march around the city seven times, and the priests shall blow the trumpets.*" (Josh.6:2-27) The final dictum represents veneration; "*You shall not shout nor let your voice be heard, nor let a word proceed out of your mouth, until the day I tell you, 'Shout'! Then you shall shout.*'"

Faithfully, Joshua led the people of Israel to the surety of conquering Jericho; each day obediently following the dictates of The Lord God. At dawn on the seventh day, they marched around the city seven times – the priests blew the trumpets – and the people shouted – and then the walls came tumbling down.

Once again, we are addressed with another principle of living by faith. At times we are given to 'praise God' prior to the miracle. We give God the glory, by faith, for what He is about to do.

On the heels of this supernatural event, we are set back on our heels. From victory at Jericho to defeat at Ai! How can such tragedies happen? Disobedience! It comes in the form of living in the natural, living by sight, living for self-gratification, among others! God had commanded the people not to covet any belonging from the city. He said, "*The city shall be under the ban,*" *the* "silver and gold *and Iron are holy to the Lord; they shall go into the treasury of the Lord.*" How could this not be understood, the directive seemed quite clear. Of course, it was clear. A man by the name of Achan: perhaps the only reason we are introduced to him is because of his impropriety. (Imagine being remembered only due to wrongdoing).

Perhaps, at first, all was well with Achan's heart; then lust captured his resolve; he coveted the gold; he justified himself; he convinced himself that somehow, he deserved the bounty;

he stole some goods under the ban. Perhaps what he didn't grasp is the fact that God's warning extended beyond the individual but the act "*would make the camp of Israel accursed and bring trouble upon it.*" Get this! The sin of one caused "*the anger of the Lord* to be *burned against the sons of Israel.*" (Josh.7:1) *If you are saying, 'that doesn't seem fair', you do not understand the basic fundamental of obedience to God's will. – without question*.

The aftermath resulted in a great defeat by Ai, which should have been taken easily. Because Israel is thwarted in the battle, the guilty recognized their sin confessing, "*Truly, I have sinned against the Lord, this is what I did: when I saw among the spoil a beautiful mantle from Shinar and two hundred shekels of silver and a bar of gold fifty shekels in weight, I coveted them and took them; you will find them concealed in dirt under my tent.*" As blessed as we might be due to Achan's admittance of his transgression, consequences would, nevertheless, be administered. The punishment affected his entire family (Josh.7:20-26).

Lessons learned through defeat.

Because of a lack of faith, we can experience defeat; but we do not return to our beginning. After the defeat at Ai, the people were not required to go back and defeat Jericho again, they proceeded from the point of the defeat.

When our failures are properly dealt with, they can be the next step to success.

Every detection of an un-truth discovered through God's Holy Spirit can lead us to absolute truth.

When walking in the flesh is detected and change is wrought, our walking in righteousness is manifested by our faith.

My Personal "Walk by Faith" Journal: Ch. 9

1. Has there been a time in your life in which you were "being trained" as someone in your life was "being tested" in a similar way that Joshua was trained while Moses was being tested?

___

___

In what way/ways did that experience help you in upcoming tests of your faith?

___

___

2. In your 'faith walk', have you found it harder to:

   a. "Wait" on God to "detail out the steps" for you to take.

___

___

or; Harder to move toward the test in faith, “getting your feet wet”, thereby, prompting God to “initiate the remaining steps”?

3. Rehab is a good example of how, at times, it takes great courage to live by faith and walk in obedience to God.

Have you in the past or are you currently facing a situation in which you need to exercise a great deal of courage to be obedient to what you know God desires of you?

If in the past, what did you do?

What were the final results?

___

___

If current. What do you plan to do?

___

___

What do you expect God will do if you take this step of faith and obedience?

___

___

4. Why is it good to give God glory and praise, as an act of faith, prior to God answering your prayers?

___

___

5. Think back to a time in which, because of a lack of faith, you suffered defeat.

___

___

How did you deal with that defeat?

____

____

What did you learn from the defeat that will aid in taking that "next step to victory"?

____

____

CHAPTER TEN

Heb. 11: 32 – 34

" Faith Flows from The Least Expected "

"What more shall I say? For time will fail me if I tell of Gideon, Barak, Samson, Jephthah, of David and Samuel and the prophets, who by faith conquered kingdoms, performed acts of righteousness, shut the mouths of lions, quenched the power of fire, escaped the edge of the sword, from weakness were made strong, became mighty in war, put forth foreign armies to flight."

Up to this point in his thesis, the author of Hebrews has accented people of faith adding some details concerning their dedication to the Lord. Now he identifies more faithful servants without those components; these are not less important or less effective; he just didn't have 'time' to, specifically, or embellish the deeds of these men of faith (Heb.11:32). We will allow Gideon to represent the feats of the five Judges listed; then include some of the accomplishments of King David; then capitalize Daniel to characterize the prophets.

Note: I believe the theme verse of the Book of Judges is found in 17: 6. "*Every man did what was right in their own eyes.*" With this as a theology, addressing anything representing theWill of God, would be taken as an offense of character and subject to persecution.

Gideon:

God gives us another exemplification of how He often patterns His step-by-step process of strengthening our walk-in faith. How He chooses to use those who grow from available - to faithful.

"Israel was brought very low because of Midian, and the sons of Israel cried out to the Lord." (Jud.6:6-8:35) Masters of Agriculture and herds, the Israelites toiled to produce and sustain the needs of the people. This was to no avail, however, for the lazy enemy would pillage the resources designed for God's citizenry. In their "cry" to the Lord, they had no idea how God would answer their supplication - perhaps, especially Gideon; for God found him *"beating out wheat in the wine press"*. That was no place to thresh wheat - no wind to separate the wheat from the chaff.

"The angel of the Lord appeared to him and said to him, 'The Lord is with you, o valiant warrior." Gideon questioned the guest, the Lord, by wanting to know why they were being abandoned. Where are all the miracles we've heard about - why are we under siege? Again, the *"Lord looked at him and said, 'Go in this your strength and deliver Israel from the hand of Midian. Have I not sent you?'"* Are You sure You have the right guy; my family is the least; and I'm the least in my family. Note: God was looking at Gideon's potential - one willing to go in the power and authority of God Himself. The Lord responded, *"Surely I will be with you, and you shall defeat Midian as one man."* Okay, I'll go - but I need a sign - some assurance it's me who is really called.

Signs: In Judges 6 we are enlightened by the means God brought Gideon to assure him it was assuredly *"The Lord God"* who was overseeing these portents. First, Gideon prepared a meal of lamb and unleavened bread and broth - he put them in a basket. God said to lay the meal upon a specified rock and pour out the broth - he did so. God, then, using a staff touched the meal, a fire sprang up and consumed the meat and unleavened bread. With eyes wide open, Gideon, "*Built an altar there to the Lord and named it The Lord Is Peace*".

Second, a test requires courageous and conclusive faith. "*Pull down the altar of Baal which belongs to your father, and the Asherah beside it; and build an altar to the Lord your God*". This action brought about much in the way of resistance from the people, even threats of death. It seems Gideon presumed the anger he would face yet carried out the Lord's request.

Third, Gideon, again, desires to re-establish God's call to take out the Midianites so he tells the Lord he will place a "*fleece of wool on the threshing floor.*" If there is dew on the wool yet the floor is dry in the morning,_I will know You have chosen me to deliver Israel. Sure enough, in the morning he examined the wool, and it was wet with dew and the floor was free of moisture. So that's proof, right? Sorry! Gideon must have deliberated the situation and concluded that, of course the wool would still be wet, and the floor dry because it would take longer for the fleece to dry. So, let's do this again! <u>* We can't avoid being amazed by the patience of the Lord.</u> *

Gideon approaches the Lord adding, "*Do not let Thine anger burn against me so that I may speak once more.*" This time allows the floor to be filled with dew and the woolen fleece completely dry. It was reasonable thinking for this, would be, servant of the Lord that still held shades of doubt. Astonishingly, "*God did so that night, for it was dry only on the fleece, and dew was on all the ground.*"

Gideon is now ready to submit to God's will for him. Wouldn't we like to think our response to His will wouldn't have been so intense or had taken such time and effort – honestly though, it most likely would have. Gideon's heart still needs perfecting, so God will take him through a process where he must yield totally to God's course of action, forsaking his own reasoning of the battle strategy.

It's time for the battle to begin and a call is sent out to the fighting men, thirty-two thousand respond to the call. I can't help wondering how Gideon is feeling due to the fact that the number of the enemy is about one hundred twenty thousand (Jud.8:10).

Gideon, 'Ok, a ratio of about four to one, I can work with that'.

Then God said, "*The people who are with you are too many for Me to give Midian into their hands, lest Israel become boastful, saying, "my own power has delivered me*"". Ask the men if any are afraid and trembling, if so, let them go home.

Twenty-two thousand? Really? Now there are only ten thousand! Is Gideon thinking, 'sure hope God is fighting this battle; the ration now is about twelve to one'.

Then God said, "*The people are still too many.*"

Gideon was to lead the people down to the water, survey carefully, and separate the men who lap up the water like a dog apart from those who kneel to drink by cupping water in their hands and bringing it to their mouth. Separation finished! Three hundred! Really? Please, God create Uzis or PULS Rockets?

God now has Gideon right where He wants/needs him to be – the same place God needs us to be – totally ready to respond to God's plan without questioning or disputing – knowing full well his wisdom has no problem-solving answers for the occasion. <u>*Faith in action*</u>

We can comfortably conclude; Gideon never would have conceived God's stratagem. Through the dream of a friend, Gideon divulged the scheme for victory. By faith, he divided the three hundred men into three companies and gave them trumpets and empty pitchers – inside the pitcher's torches were placed. He surrounded the Midian army with his men instructing them to blow the trumpets and break the lighted pitchers and shout "A *sword for the Lord and for Gideon.*" (Jud.7:10-22) Then the Lord "*set the sword of one against another even throughout the whole army; and the army fled.*" <u>One hundred twenty thousand swordsmen fell that day!</u>

King David:

There is no way we can exhaust the faith life of David in this publication. We will endeavor to unveil both faithful victories and wavering examples; plus, I don't suppose any of us would relish our lives being an open book as David's.

Due to the unfaithfulness of king Saul, "*the Spirit of the Lord departed from Saul*" and it became time for God to choose his replacement. David filled the bill for it is written that David, "*was a skillful musician, a mighty man of valor, a warrior, one prudent in speech, and a handsome man; and* (most important) *the Lord is with him.*" (1 Sam.16:14,18) Without delay, David would have an opportunity to prove that the 'Lord was with him' (1 Sam.17).

David entered the valley of Elah bringing supplies to his brothers as his father had commanded him. What he found was the Philistines on one side of the valley and the ranks of Israel on the other. No fighting – just taunting! The Philistines were elated because their nine foot plus guy, Goliath, was in charge, making his way down to the valley floor. Shouting and sneering and provoking insults at Saul's army. "*Why do you come out…in a battle array? Am I not a Philistine and you are servants of Saul? Choose a man for yourselves and let him come down to me. If he is able to fight me and kill me, then we will be your servants; but if I prevail against him and kill him, then you shall become our servants and serve us. I defy the ranks of Israel.*" (1 Sam.17:1-47)

Alas, while the Philistines are elated – the Israelites are "*dismayed and greatly afraid,*" for no-one was found with the courage to fight the giant. Instead, they fled the scene! David witnessing the events couldn't believe what he was observing, and became quite vocal, even at the rebuke of his brother, Eliab. "*Who is this uncircumcised Philistine, that he should taunt the armies of God?*" *David then* approached Saul saying, "*Let no man's heart fail on account of him; your servant will go and fight with this Philistine.*"

Saul rejected the idea, concluding the obvious – you're too young and frail. David espoused his skills relating to his victory over a lion and a bear and assured Saul the giant would succumb to the same fate. Saul relented and clad David with his own armor, but he rejected them and took them off. Instead, he chose five stones as his weapons, and armed with his sling, he neared the enemy who was mouthing vicious ridicule.

"*You come to me with a sword, a spear, and a javelin, but I come to you in the Name of the Lord of hosts, the God of the armies of Israel, whom you have taunted. This day the Lord will deliver you up into my hands, and I will strike you down and remove your head from you.*" David added that they all might "*know that the Lord does not deliver by sword or by spear; for the battle is the Lord's.*" Well, I think we all know that David prevailed – the giant was dead, and his head severed. When the Philistines saw what had happened, they hightailed it in great fear.

> Evaluating the circumstances; then devising a plan based on the particulars, will hinder actions that result in functions of 'faith' every time. One's visual perception accompanied by one's experience is most often misinterpreted, that leads to conclusions that are of 'self' or the 'flesh'. Saul's answers were based on this principle. The Israelites and Philistines both were guilty. The Israelites in earthly fear. The Philistines in earthly confidence. The name of the Lord evicts fear and reinforces confidence. Faith is allowing God to interpret and conceive the victory plan.

Unfortunately, not all of David's decisions bring about the glories of living by faith. We just need to be reminded of his lack of judgment when it came to Bathsheba. David's first mistake was when he failed to be where he was designed to be. "*At the time when kings go out to battle...but David stayed in Jerusalem.*" (2 Sam.11:1-17) As a result, he was in his house on, supposedly, a warm night; so, he went out on the terrace and beheld a woman bathing, who appeared beautiful. Instead of fleeing the temptation, and going back to bed, he yielded to the temptation. "*He sent and inquired about the woman...and sent messengers...and lay with her.*" Another lack of judgment!

Word came to David from Bathsheba saying, "*I am pregnant.*" Now what? Oh, I know! I'll arrange the circumstances where I "*place Uriah,* (Bathsheba's husband) *in the front line of the fiercest battle and withdraw from him, so that he may be struck down and die.*" His plan worked and Uriah died – now they could marry. (Let me insert; thankfully, abortion was not an option.)

As Paul Harvey used to say, "Now the rest of the story."

David knew he stood guilty before the Lord God. Now, what to do? What does one do when guilt presses upon the soul? Especially one who, it is said to be a "*man after God's own heart?* Confess! Manifest a penitent heart! Plead before "*The Great I Am*" a prayer of contrition covering the transgression as displayed in Psalm 51. <u>By faith;</u> David's entreaty acknowledged God's "*lovingkindness*" and the "*greatness of His compassion*" – that he would be "*washed thoroughly*" and "*cleansed from his sin.*"

By faith; he was able to advocate that "*purifications with hyssop*" assured he "**shall be clean,"** and that when "*washed*" he "***shall be whiter than snow***." By faith; he could cry out, "*Create in me a clean heart, O God, and renew a steadfast spirit within me..... Restore to me the joy of my salvation.*"

Our prayer life is Faith in action. When "*we confess our sin, He is faithful and righteous to forgive us our sins and to cleanse us from all unrighteousness.*" (1 Jn.1:9) We are drawn to the confidence and affirmation that our humble soul encounters when on our knees. Jesus taught, "*Therefore I say to you, all things for which you pray and ask, believe you have received them, and they shall be granted you,*" (Mk.11:24) In James the church is exhorted to, when sick, *call for the Elders – let them pray – and the prayer offered in faith will restore the one who is sick.*" (Jms.5:13-18) Elijah is an example given of praying in faith believing. The rain stopped as a result if his prayer and started again upon the request made in prayer. Essentially, our first prayer with meaning is when we pray "for *by grace we are saved through faith, not of ourselves, it is a gift of God.*"

Our hearts are cleansed by faith. (Acts 15: 9) Justification is by faith. (Rom 5:1)

Prophet Daniel:

Undoubtedly, we could chronicle any of the prophets given in the scriptures. Why Daniel? I suppose a preference for one, but with our minds reflecting on prayer, Daniel stands out as a man of great faith and an intense prayer warrior.

One of the principles of faith we exercise is that of establishing commitments to live by in our faith walk with Christ. When restraints are entered into, we are unsure of what the future holds and how unpredictable events might alter our resolve – but we fashion these as obligations before the Lord and, by faith, maintain our determination to live victoriously no matter what.

Such a commitment was composed by Daniel in stating "*that he would not defile himself with the king's choice food* (highly probable food offered to idols) *or with the wine he drank.*" (Dan.1:4-16) King Nebuchadnezzar believed he had the plan to ensure his appointed men would mature into the assistants he needed to serve in his court. Thus, the requirements regarding their diet and education and physical attractiveness. Daniel didn't agree though, inciting his proposal to the commander in charge.

He was officially granted favor in allowing he and his three friends to dine on vegetables and water for ten days. At the end of the ten days, they were to be compared to the others who had feasted on the king's best. Sure enough, ten days had elapsed and the appearance of the four "*seemed better and they were fatter than all the youths who had been eating the king's food.*" (So much for thinking that vegetarians are skinnier!) God blessed Daniel's steadfastness and "*the overseer continued to withhold their choice food....and kept giving them vegetables.*" Also, God "*gave them knowledge and intelligence in every branch of literature and wisdom; Daniel even understood all kinds of visions and dreams."*

It wasn't long before Daniel's gifts of "*understanding... visions and dreams*" were required. King Nebuchadnezzar "*had a dream... and his spirit was anxious to understand.*" He was prompted to engage his "*magicians, sorcerers, and conjurers*" to interpret his dream; not only, could they not give an answer but stated, "*There is not a man on earth who could declare* the *matter to the king.*" Daniel then related the matter to his three friends. They all beseeched the "*God of heaven*" for an answer to the dilemma. That day Daniel was given the solution in a "*night vision*"; he countered by testifying that "*the name of God be blessed forever and ever, for wisdom and power belong to Him.*"

Daniel assured the King Nebuchadnezzar it was God who had given the interpretation; then divulged the particulars to him. Presented were declarations, the likes of, which had never been divulged before. Prophetic mysteries that, most assuredly, would come to pass. Not absolutely convinced that he fully comprehended the impact of the message, for him, or the future, but he was so taken back he "*fell on his face and <u>did homage to Daniel</u>*", further adding, "*Surely your God is a God of gods and a Lord of kings and a revealer of mysteries.*"

Allow me to sidestep for a moment:

As I study this passage, I'm impressed the king didn't "*pay homage to God*", *but Daniel.* These Scriptural revelations are monumental and personal to the true believer, they who are, with anticipation, endeavoring to discern God's activities in the "last days" and looking intently of Christ's return for His Bride. I'm of the persuasion that Nebuchadnezzar didn't get it. If he had, it seems his future choices would have espoused godliness. What illuminates from the text in Daniel chapters 3 & 4, the king was seeking worship directed to himself rather than the "god' he spoke of. He "*made an image of gold*" some ninety feet tall and nine feet wide, then sent out a declaration that at certain times all were to "*fall down and worship the golden image the king had set up*" And, "*whoever does not fall down, and worship shall be cast into the midst of a furnace of burning fire.*" (Da. 3:1-30)

This, of course, leads into the account including Shadrach, Meshach and Abeb-nego. The three friends of Daniel who "*disregarded*" the king's orders, for they would "*not serve your gods or worship the golden image which you have set up.*" 'Then you must suffer the consequences!' "*If it be so, our God we serve will be able to deliver us from the furnace of blazing fire...But, even if He does not, let it be known to you, O king, that we are not going to serve your gods or worship the golden image you have set up.*" This is 'walking by faith' to the max! These "*servants of the Most High God*" were unscathed by the fire; in fact, there wasn't even a trace of smoke on their clothes. Their faith was incredibly and miraculously honored by God's presence.

I walk down this path to share a truth I believe God has revealed. We are in the 'last days' – we are enlightened by the truth of witnessing the above teaching repeating itself today. In our nation's capital there are those in high places who are replicating actions similar to Nebuchadnezzar. They give reference to 'god' by making statements like, "God bless America." Then they fabricate mandates that true believers cannot conform to and must be 'disregarded'. Then those proposing to follow their Lord are subject to persecution – the consequences. I submit, their reference to deity is accenting "god" – for I ask, "What God are you referring too? Must be "god" with a small 'G' – not a capitol "G" for "God". The Most High God would never ask His Children to succumb to Abortion, or Gay and Trans-gender lifestyles, Equity, amid other ungodly precepts. Those in control are not bringing glory to God - but themselves – they desire the worship of control.

The further from God's truth this culture falls; the more faith will be required of His Children!

In Daniel chapter six another similar illustration is presented. Daniel's character was so pronounced in distinguishing ways, Darius "*planned to appoint him over the entire kingdom.*" The evil political competition heard about the plan and set out to accuse him! Of what? Don't know yet, but we'll find something! After searching for a reason, they thought we'll bring action "*with regard to the law of his God.*" They knew their religion differed from Daniel's beliefs.

An "*injunction*" by king Darius was drawn up and signed. No one is to "*make a petition to any god or man beside you.*" Daniel knew the document was signed, and the ramifications of it; yet he "*continued kneeling on his knees three times a day, praying and giving thanks before his God.*" (Dan.6:1-28) Comprehending the magnitude of his actions, not only aware of being thrown into the lions' den for thirty days, but his execution of insubordination against authority. Both requiring great faith :

1. Believing that God would "*shut the lions' mouths...and no harm,*" which He did.
2. Protection from those would-be assassinations due to his rebellion against the government.

Much of the remaining teaching in Daniel focuses on the "last days". Events that will take place after the "rapture" of the church.

Before that event is set in place, we believers might be asked to endure some intense ungodly decisions made by those in authority.

Our faith will be tested! Are we ready?

My Personal "Faith Walk" Journal: Ch. 10

1. In what ways can you relate to Gideon and his call from the Lord in terms of the following?

a. Feeling inadequate regarding God's call on your life.

____

____

b. Feeling you need a sign from God prior to moving forward.

____

____

c. In need of courage to do the right thing, knowing there will be opposition.

____

____

d. In need of a 'fleece' for further assurance concerning God's will.

____

____

e. Or, you say, I'm totally ready to respond to God's plan without question or disputes.

____

____

2. The lion and bear that David had previously killed, with God's help, were faith builders that increased David's faith and courage to fight Goliath.

____

____

What "faith builders" are in your past that can help you, with great confidence, face any Goliath's in your life?

____

____

3. There are lessons to be learned from David's sin with Bathsheba that can strengthen our own faith walk; if we can/will take them to heart.

____

____

Sin can be, and mostly is, a very slippery slope. One transgression can set into motion a chain of sinful events that can cover up, or over-shadow, the original sin.

Have you experienced this in your past?

____

____

How did you overcome and get off that "slippery slope"?

____

____

Are you considering that no matter the sin, God's grace is more than sufficient when "*we confess our sins*, knowing, *He is faithful and righteous to forgive us our sins and cleanse us from all unrighteousness.*" (1 Jn.1:9)

If you are sensing that the Holy Spirit is dealing with your heart, prompting you to confess sin in your life, stop right here and spend some time praying for restoration of your broken heart before Him.

4. Prayer was a vital and key factor In Daniel's daily faith walk (Dan.6:10). In terms of priorities in your daily life, where does prayer fall?

____

____

How much of your day is devoted fully to prayer and time alone in meditation with the Lord?

____

____

5. As we witness a continuing falling away from Godliness, our culture is suffering from distancing itself from God's truths and a Biblical worldview. The author states that a deeper faith will be required, in this erosion of unrighteousness, for God's Children to live righteously.

What does that mean for you and your faith walk?

____

____

What can you do to strengthen your faith, so that you do not end up succumbing to cultural pressures so prevalent in our day?

____

____

CHAPTER ELEVEN

Heb. 11: 35 - 40

" Ultimate Living for People of Faith "

“Women received back their dead by resurrection; and others were ***tortured, not accepting their release, in order*** that they might obtain a better resurrection; ***and others exper***ienced ***mockings and scourgings, yes, also chains and imprisonment. They were stoned, they were sawn in two, they were tempted, they were put to death with the sword; they went about in sheepskins, in goatskins, being destitute, afflicted, illtreated (men of whom the world is not worthy), wondering in deserts and mountains***

and caves and holes in the ground. And all these, having gained approval through their faith, did not receive what was promised, because God had provided something better for us, so that apart from us they should not be made perfect."

Upon finishing the copy of the above portion of Scripture, I sat in awe reflecting on the level of faith the people maintained as they were tested for consistency and endurance. Some examples given in the text includes:

* Elijah: (1 Kings 17: 1-24) Elijah stood before the people saying, 'I have a weather report,' "*there will be neither* dew nor rain these years." During that three-year drought Elijah was sent to the widow, Zarephath and her son; for God had warned her of the encounter. Elijah said to her, "*bring me a little water*...and *a piece of bread.*" She responded. "I *have no bread....only some flour...and some oil*" I was going to prepare a meal for me and my son. "*That we may eat it and die.*" *Elijah said,* "*Do not fear – make a little for me first, bring it to me – then you can make some for you and your son.*" God has said that neither "*The bowl of flour*" nor "*the jar of oil*" will be depleted until the drought is past. We have no idea what went through her mind or how long she would mull it over; all we know is that she "*did according to the word of Elijah.*" As we examine the text further, we read of the tragedy of her son's death. She seems to blame Elijah but gives him over to be ministered to by Elijah. Elijah promptly called out the Lord on the sons' behalf and God heard his plea and healed the boy. The faith of Elijah spilled over and inspired the mom to live in faith.

* Jeremiah: (Jere. 1: 4-19; 20:1-10) The "*word of the Lord came*" to Jeremiah appointing him to prophecy against the sins of the people. Reminiscent of Moses, he rebutted by saying, "I *do not know how to speak*" and "I *am a youth.*" But God assured him "*He would put words into his mouth*" and ever be with him. As we survey the biblical account, we find that, even though Jeremiah is reluctant, he obeys. He preaches God's word! But the people resist the messages and impose their displeasure by having him "*beaten* and *put him in stocks.*" It's amazing that in his state of insecurity he presses on. Even though he proclaims he is "*a laughingstock*" and "*mocked.*" And "*cries aloud*" *and* "*in reproach and derision all day long,*" Yet he *remains* faithful to his calling. The proclamation of the message was more important than the abuse it might produce! Faith in action!

* Zachariah (2 Chron.24:17-21) This account represents a time when the people "*abandoned the house of the Lord, the God of their fathers, and served the Asherim and the idols.*" So, God sent prophets "*to bring them back to the Lord....but they would not listen.*" But God wasn't through reaching out to them and "*the Spirit of God* came on Zachariah *the son of Jehoiada the priest,*"_ We are not very familiar with this Zachariah, but he "*stood above the people and said, 'Why do you transgress the commandments of the Lord? You have forsaken the Lord!* Listen: "*He has forsaken you!* Consistent with human nature, the people became angered and "*conspired against him...and they stoned him to death in the house of the Lord.*" How honoring to our God!

* Stephen (Acts 7:1-8:1) A true hero of walking by faith is Stephen. He finds himself before members of the court and

proceeds with his defense. Not for acquittal, but to present truth the leaders needed to hear for failing to recognize Jesus Christ as The True Messiah. At times truth can produce negative responses from those being confronted with it; as it did here. Especially when Stephen sharply directed his comments to the *"men who are stiff-necked and uncircumcised in heart...resisting the Holy Spirit."* Stephen gazing into the heavens witnessed *"the heavens open and the Son of Man standing at the right hand of God."* The belligerent self-righteous men sought revenge by stoning him to death. We wonder how convicting it was for these men to hear Stephen assert, *"Lord, do not hold this sin against them!"*

The above illustrates just a few of the many accounts we have in Scripture who exercised a life of faith in their response to God's call upon their lives. The Apostles of Christ have similar narrations in their lives; we find them in the Scriptures; they include:

* James: (Acts 12: 1,2) The movement of God was incredible covering the early years of the church, the assassination of Stephen didn't affect the growth of the people or the organism. It continued flourishing, I'm sure, to the chagrin of Satan. Perhaps the old devil thought, "I know threats of persecution cast upon the members can discourage the most dedicated to the cause; especially if it's directed toward their leadership." With this as a possibility, it is little wonder that James; the brother of John; one of the twelve; one of the three in the inner circle of the Lord Jesus who would be chosen to suffer; for no apparent reason, other than he *"belonged to the church"* and must be *"mistreated."* Thus,

Herod, the Hitler of the day, ordered him to be "*put to death with a sword.*"

* Peter: (Acts 12: 3-19) While the church was agonizing over the death of James, the Jews were rejoicing. Herod wallowed in his decisions to disrupt all he could. Thus, he had another leader, Peter, arrested and imprisoned. (This wasn't the first incarceration for Peter for he had shared cells with John on previous occasions – Acts 4, 5) Herod, not wanting to take any chances had him watched by "*two soldiers, bound with two chains; and guards*" watching the front gate. His plan back-fired, however, because God intervened, and freed him.

* Paul: (Acts 16:11-33) Chronicling all of Paul's encounters with suffering would take a book of its own. One example is found in Acts 16; as usual, the religious people of the day rejected 'truth' they needed to hear. The result was that "*the crowd rose up against them*" (Paul and Silas); "*tore their robes off*" and they were "*beaten with rods.*" Next, they were "*thrown into the inner prison, and fastened their feet in the stocks.*" In a way to expedite our study and yet cover the suffering of Paul for Christ, we read "*Five times I received from the Jews thirty-nine lashes. Three times I was beaten with rods, once I was stoned, three times I was shipwrecked, a night and a day I have spent in the deep. I have been on frequent journeys, in danger from rivers. dangers from robbers, dangers from my countrymen, dangers from the Gentiles, dangers from the city, dangers in the wilderness, dangers on the sea, dangers among false brethren; I have been in labor and hardship, through many sleepless nights, in hunger and thirst, often without food, in cold and exposure.*" (2 Cor.11:23-27) Ultimately, Paul was martyred, by beheading, in Rome by Nero.

There are reports and legends that abound relevant to the persecution of the Disciples of Jesus. These can be found in a myriad of places, but are not always reliable, so I've only presented examples from God's Word. This is not to say, they didn't experience inhumane grief, nor that they did not meet with violent deaths. The call of the Master was upon their lives. The message of salvation through Jesus the Christ, being the only way to the Father, was imprinted upon their mind and heart. If they didn't carry the "Good News" who would? Make no mistake, they knew of the dangers set before them; they also knew they were in the hands of an Omnipotent Sovereign God; nothing, nor anyone could touch them unless God allowed it. Safe and secure they were until their ministries were completed – when it was time to receive them into God's presence. Why did they submit? There is nothing greater than the call of God in life.

We've received the same call! Jesus prayed for them and us by stating, "*I do not ask on behalf of these alone, but for those who believe in Me through their word.*". (Jn.17:20)

Question is: are we willing to submit?

We are privileged to have examples of those who get it – today. People who are willing to stand against the tide. Who, actually, believes the Amendments of our Constitution and favors challenging those who suppress the freedoms they endorse. With regret we must question the truth of the statements made regarding "freedom." Is it freedom when Students who have been censored for drawing attention to our Lord Jesus embedded in their graduation remarks? Is it freedom when "bakers of cakes" are scrutinized for choosing not to accommodate worldly views? Is it freedom when one's "spiritual convictions to witness" are disallowed in the workplace? Is it freedom when we are obliged to forgo our "Biblical creeds" and compromise values we've been taught to honor? We praise our Lord when folks revolt against the flow and authenticate their faith.

Why the emphasis on how God's people have been tyrannized through the ages? Jesus was bruised, beaten, and crucified so we could secure "*Eternal Life.*" When we identify with Him *spiritually*, we must be willing to identify with Him *physically*. Jesus puts it this way, "*Blessed are those who have been persecuted for the sake of righteousness, for theirs is the kingdom of heaven. Blessed are you when men cast insults at you, and persecute you, and say all kinds of evil against you falsely, on account of Me. Rejoice and be glad, for your reward in heaven is great, for so they persecuted the prophets who were before you.*" (Mt.5:10-12) Yes! This takes great faith!

Perhaps one of the greatest tests for living by faith is the emphasis we place upon "*He who loves his life ... in this world;*" for he will "*lose it;*" conversely, for "*he who hates his life in this world shall keep it to life eternal.*" (Jn. 12:25) Then couple these statements of Paul's assessments when he states, "*To live is Christ, to die is gain,*" (Phil.1:21) We enjoy the confidence and assurance that the last breath we take on this earth will usher us into God's presence – with no fear.

One's salvation equates to "Eternal Life." This life is but a vapor compared to eternity. We must question ourselves as to why there is such momentous stress in worldly achievements.

Biblical faith is not about *"building up treasures on earth"* where 'things' can be destroyed, but *"lay up treasures in heaven where"* nothing can *"destroy"*. (Mt.6:19,29) The more 'treasures' we have in heaven the more we will look forward to being in our Lord's presence.

We can end our study by reading the words of Esther K. Rusthoi - 1940 **"*It will be worth it all."***

Sometimes the day seems long, our trials hard to bear. We're tempted to complain, to murmur and despair.

But Christ will soon appear to catch His bride away! All tears forever over in God's eternal day!

It will be worth it all when we see Jesus! Life's trials seem so small when we see Christ. One glimpse of His dear face, all sorrow will erase. So, bravely run the race til we see Christ.

Life's day will soon be o're, all storms forever past;

We'll cross the great divide too Glory, safe at last! We'll share the joys of heaven, a harp, a home, a crown.The tempter will be ***banished, we'll lay our burdens down.***

It will be worth it all when we see Jesus! Life's trials seem so small when we see Christ. One glimpse of His dear face, all sorrow will erase. So bravely run the race til we see Christ.

My Personal "Faith" walk – Journal: Chapter 11

1. There are several very positive examples in Scripture of people who remained strong and put their faith into action as they were "tested with consistency and endurance" during times of suffering and persecution.

Which of those examples have you found to be an encouragement to you when you find yourself going through difficult times?

____

____

What have you specifically learned from their example that has helped you to be able to put your faith into action?

____

____

2. We read in God's Word how the early church continues to grow during such times of great persecution. We read today how Christianity is significantly growing in other countries such as Afghanistan, North Korea, Iran, China, and Nigeria despite intense persecution. Young and old suffering to the point of and including death.

This fact seems to suggest that the more Christians suffer for their faith, the more the church grows - as well as the personal faith of the members.

Do you believe this to be the case? If so, why?

____

____

Why does suffering and persecution often cause the church to grow?

____

____

What about individuals in those situations also growing in their faith.

____

____

3. In the 'Parable of the Sower' (Matt.13: 20.21); one discovers that the seed that fell on "*rocky* ground" refers to someone "*who hears the Word, and immediately receives it with joy*". But it has no root, therefore it is only temporary; "*when* affliction and persecution arise because of the word, immediately (they) fall away." This passage suggests that there are some who, instead of growing stronger in their faith, "fall" away from their faith.

How about you? As we are experiencing more and more of our Christian freedoms being suppressed here in America, are you personally prepared to suffer for your faith?

____

____

If not, what might you do to become better prepared for times of intense persecution that appears to be headed for Christians here in this Country?

____

____

4. Take some time to, carefully and honestly, reflect back on how you used your <u>time</u>, your <u>talent</u>, and your <u>treasure</u> (financial resources) over the past six to twelve months. Upon doing this, would you say that your priorities have been more focused upon "*building up treasures in heaven or building upon treasures on earth?*

If more on earth; what steps are you going to take to become more "heavenly" minded? To focus upon building treasures that are everlasting and will not "fade away." Meditating on Mt. 6:21 that states: *"for where your treasure is, there will your heart be also."*

* The date of my reading of these Biblical principles: __________My four commitments I make to the Lord and will check on how I'm "growing in my faith walk" consistently.

1.

____

____

2.

____

____

3.

____

____

4.

____

____

About the Author

Arlin Sanford

I was very blessed to be born into a family where 'faith' was demonstrated in many ways. It was mentored and taught to me the importance of living by 'faith' and not by sight. Over the years I've found myself, at times, floundering in my faith; but then there have been times when the mentoring and teaching actually brought victory. Praise the Lord for the latter.

Our many years spent in the Pastoral Ministry have been challenging at times. "Living by faith" has become more than just a saying – it's become a summons to exercise true belief. Thus, it's not unusual to experience periods of defeat – but when victory comes, it's all the more satisfying. It's worth every minute of the journey.

God has blessed my wife Lana and myself with four children, 13 grandchildren, and 26 great-grandchildren. The very thought makes me "quiver" (Psalm 127). Believe me, opportunities to exercise faith are endless. God has been incredibly steadfast in His faithfulness.

Perhaps you weren't blessed with such examples; your story takes on a different direction. But, as I have experienced, the reading and study of God's Word will ignite and fortify your faith and you can be empowered through the Holy Spirit to rise above every situation you might face.

God bless you on your journey – and for your victories.

Made in the USA
Columbia, SC
24 November 2023